W. G. GRACE

IN THE STEPS OF A LEGEND

ANTHONY MEREDITH

A grateful salute to the memory of Frank Vigar, Sonny Avery and Bill Dines,
wonderful coaches and fine cricketers who exuded a love of the game.

First published 2015
This edition published 2017

Amberley Publishing
The Hill, Stroud
Gloucestershire, GL5 4EP

www.amberley-books.com

British Library Cataloguing in Publication Data.
A catalogue record for this book is available from the British Library.

ISBN 978-1-4456-5959-6 (paperback)
ISBN 978-1-4456-1796-1 (ebook)

Origination by Amberley Publishing.
Printed in the UK.

Contents

Acknowledgements

Very many thanks to Jenny Stephens and Jenna Whittle for all their administrations at Amberley; to Elizabeth Watts, who was helpful along the way; and Joe Pettican, who encouraged the original idea. It is surely appropriate that a book marking the centenary of W.G. Grace's death should be published by a company based at Stroud, close to so many of W.G.'s happiest Gloucestershire hunting grounds. W.G., indeed, was once the star attraction in a low-scoring match at Stroud back in 1882, when his cousin's United Eleven of All-England played Twenty-two of Stroud and District.

I am also very grateful to Barry Aitken, Minhal Al Halabi, Katherine Arnold, Laurie Baker, Simon Balderson, Phil Barnes, Sam Beavis, Commander Geoffrey Bond, Andy Buchan, Adam Chadwick, Ken Clarke, Andrew Collier, Daniel Collings, Robert Curphey, Anita Dobson, Noel Dures, Jon Filby, Alan Freke, Roger Gibbons, Robin Taylor Gilbert, Anselm Guise, Ricky Gunn, Paul Harris, Keith Hunt, Col. Duncan Hyslop, Rob Johnson, Peter Jouning, John Kennett, Andy King, Jack Lillywhite, Roger Long, John Longstaff, Anne Maguire, Charlotte Markham, Rosemary Marryatt, Trevor Norman, Carl Openshaw, Max Parkin, Minesh Patel, Bob Pigeon, Andrew Plaster, Steve Powell, Bryan Rawlings, Keith Rees, David Robinson, Neil Robinson, Nicholas Sharp, Rebecca Sillence, Howard Smith, Mark Stickings, Canon Christopher Sugden, Les Summerfield, Philippa Threlfall, John Walker and Margaret and Roy Walker.

Many thanks, too, to the Bristol Records Office, the Cheltenham Local & Family History Library, Christ Church (Downend), the Eltham Society, the Forty Club, Gloucestershire County Cricket Club, Grimsby Reference Library, Lakes District Museum (Arrowtown, New Zealand), the Lillywhite Family Museum (Florida), the M.C.C. Library, the Museum of Bristol, Salem Methodist Church (Winterbourne), the Royal Society of Medicine Library, St James' Church (Mangotsfield) and the Sussex Cricket Museum.

Photographic sources have been indicated where known. We would be grateful to be told of any instances in which we have failed to acknowledge properly other peoples' work, despite our best intentions and efforts. Any such omissions will be rectified in any subsequent editions.

I am as ever deeply grateful to my wife Heather, who somehow smilingly coped with all the mayhem of W.G. and nobly kept Boycott, a fairly opinionated West Highland terrier, under control during various excursions; to my daughter Jo, at all times a great confidence booster; and to my brother Michael, the foundations of whose cricket were also, like mine, laid by the three dedicatees.

Anthony Meredith
Akeley, May 2015

1

A Family Reconnaissance

In search of the Graces and Pococks, 1800–48

We are nearing Bristol at the start of our exploration in the steps of cricket's greatest legend, W.G. Grace. There will be several more visits to the city, for Bristol was W.G.'s home for almost the whole of the first fifty years of his life; it is rich in Grace relics and associations.

As we turn sharply off the M4 to take the motorway leading into the city centre, a large pile of books shifts uneasily on the back seat. No other cricketer – perhaps no other sportsman – has been written about so thoroughly over so long a period. We will have plenty of helpful travelling companions.

The first biography, by Methven Brownlee, came out in 1887 when Grace was thirty-nine, with further cricket seasons still before him. Three volumes of ghosted autobiography followed: *Cricket* in 1891; the less succinctly titled *W.G.: The Cricketing Reminiscences and Personal Recollections of W.G. Grace* in 1899; and *W.G.'s Little Book* of 1909, published when he was sixty-one, a year after his last first-class game. *The Memorial Biography of Dr W.G. Grace*, sponsored by M.C.C. and published in 1919, completed this invaluable quintet – a first point of reference for all subsequent biographers.

These have included golfer Bernard Darwin (1934), two Gloucestershire devotees, Powell and Caple (1948), poet-playwright Clifford Bax (1952), humorist and sports writer A. A. Thomson (1957), social historian Eric Midwinter (1981) and journalist Robert Low (1997). In 1998 the 150th anniversary of W.G.'s birth was marked by two important additions: the 550-page, groundbreaking biography of poet and radio-presenter Simon Rae and statistician J. R. Webber's remarkable *Chronicle of W.G.*, its 1,100 pages detailing every known innings Grace played between the ages of nine and sixty-six. We shall not be travelling light.

* * *

We turn off the M32 almost as soon as we join it and head for Bristol's north-eastern outskirts. Soon there are signs to Mangotsfield, the parish in which Grace was born, and Downend, his actual place of birth and the first stop on our journey. In the mid-nineteenth century Mangotsfield and Downend were adjacent villages set deep in the Gloucestershire countryside, three miles outside the city, but they were swallowed up years ago in suburban sprawl. As we negotiate our way through the modern jumble of residential development, our back-seat library will help in recreating the past.

Methven Brownlee, for example, painted a rhapsodic picture of Victorian Downend: 'Life moves quietly and steadily there. Picturesque Frenchay, Stapleton and Frome Glen are within easy distance, and lovers of the romantic and the beautiful are to be seen most days of the week, during the spring and summer months, exploring the woods and picking the wild flowers that grow in abundance.' Old maps however, reveal that nearly all these pretty villages by the River Frome were scarred by some of the many quarries and coal mines answering the needs of Bristol's ever-growing industrialisation.

Modern Downend boasts many Grace mementoes; we are contenting ourselves on this visit with just three. As we drive up Cleeve Hill to a small roundabout in front of the Willows Shopping Centre, we are closing in on one of the most striking – a ceramic mural. There he is, the bearded cricket champion. Located on top of a single-storey red-brick shopping development, where he has been since the early 1980s, staring directly across the roundabout and down North Street towards two houses that vie as his birthplace. Resplendent in his M.C.C. cap, Grace sits in front of his Downend home with a well-used bat lying in readiness between white pads and brown boots. 'WG 1848–1915' runs the inscription beneath. He needs no surname. Even though he died so long ago, most people have still heard of W.G.

It is such a wonderfully imaginative and effective tribute that we have asked its creator, Philippa Threlfall, one of the country's leading ceramicists, to tell us a little more about it: 'My late husband and I,' she explains, 'worked initially from photographs of W.G. and illustrations of his main childhood home, The Chesnuts ... The images of W.G. and his house were modelled separately and then attached together, creating one huge clay model, which was later cut up into smaller pieces, like a stained-glass window. Then came the firing in the kiln and the glazing ...' Long may the W.G. ceramic be a source of inspiration in the lives of Downend's shoppers!

Our second objective, Downend House, is a detached, three-storeyed Georgian building, bright in its off-white stucco, on the far side of the roundabout at the corner of North Street and Salisbury Road. It was rented by W.G.'s parents for nearly twenty years, between 1831 and 1850. Here Mrs Martha Grace gave birth to all seven of W.G.'s elder brothers and sisters: Henry (1833), Annie (1834), Fanny (1838), Alfred (1840), Edward (1841), Alice (1845) and Blanche (1846). The house now features on the Kingswood Heritage Trail and, if a brass plaque on the front of the house is to be believed, 'Dr W.G. Grace, famous Gloucester cricketer, was born here, 18 July 1848.'

Because W.G. lived at Downend House for the first two years of his life, it has been assumed that he, too, was born there. However, local historian Revd Emlyn Jones categorically refuted this back in 1899: 'His sister, Mrs Henry Skelton, informed the writer that W.G. was born in the house higher up, Clematis House, where the Curate of Mangotsfield lives.' Emlyn Jones was himself the long-serving curate of Christ Church, where the Graces worshipped, just down the road from Clematis House and Downend House. W.G.'s sister, Annie Skelton, was that church's first organist, a post she held there for fifty years; her husband was one of the church wardens; her brother-in-law, the vicar. So the word of W.G.'s big sister Annie can surely be trusted. Family circumstances also support the claim. By 1848 Downend House was overrun by boisterous children. The Graces had outgrown their home and would leave it two years later for that very reason. So when the local church suggested to Martha, one of its leading choristers, that her confinement might be easier at a charming nearby church property, the Graces would have quickly closed with the offer. Although as yet it boasts no plaque, we can be sure Clematis House was W.G.'s birthplace.

* * *

We move on to the heart of the city, to explore more of the family background at the church where W.G.'s parents were married. We have skirted Temple Meads Station (opened for Brunel's Great Western Railway shortly before W.G. was born), crossed the River Avon and climbed up towards the church of St Michael's-on-the-Mount-Without, at the bottom of the steep St Michael's Hill. Alas, after serving the community for over 700 years, the fine Grade II-listed church was deemed surplus to requirements in 1999 and is now boarded up and on the Buildings at Risk register, still awaiting a new future which, in 2006, was nearly that of a shoe shop.

Prior to her marriage Martha Grace had lived next door to the church all her life, for her father, George Pocock, ran a school from his home in Prospect Place, situated directly above Lower Church Lane, under the shadow of St Michael's Tower. Prospect Place and its academy have both disappeared, a primary school car-park currently occupying part of the Pococks' property. However, an engraving survives from an old school flyer, showing a broad-fronted eighteenth-century town house of three storeys, with an additional wing for the dormitories and schoolroom housing the dozen to two-dozen pupils.

W.G.'s mother, then, had not very far to walk when, as a nineteen-year-old bride and a strapping tomboy, she emerged from Prospect Place Academy on the arm of her extrovert father, George, in November 1831, to marry a twenty-three-year-old doctor, Henry Mills Grace. Fortunately the paved walkways all around the church, high up above the traffic, help us recreate in our imaginations that happy day. As they strode towards St Michael's they caught all eyes. W.G.'s grandfather in particular cut a very striking figure: a large man of fifty-seven, clean-shaven, immaculately dressed with a messianic glint in the eyes that gave away his triple role of headmaster, inventor and missionary. He deserves our attention, for just as many of his traits of character were inherited by his daughter Martha – these in turn can be seen even more fully in his famous grandson.

Martha's wedding hymns were sung with fervour by all the Pococks. The ninth of fourteen children, she had been brought up in an atmosphere where Christian virtues were passionately inculcated alongside an equally vibrant work ethic. The single-mindedness that she was later to apply to the advancement of her husband and sons' professions took root at Prospect Place. As a child, for example, she had joined in the communal singing of the resolute hymn 'Before School Duties' to a lyric written by her father:

> Gracious Lord, I ask of thee
> Promised wisdom now impart;
> Grant thy heavenly aid to me;
> Give the understanding heart.
>
> Save me from a wandering mind;
> Keep intrusive thoughts away,
> Make me studiously inclined;
> Help me while I think, to pray.
>
> And to crown what I desire,
> Strengthen my retentive powers,
> Lest I lose what I acquire
> During more indulgent hours.

George Pocock, with his evangelical missionary zeal, would have found the closure of St Michael's unthinkable. He was in the business of opening places of worship, not closing them. Inspired by Wesleyism, Grandfather George had pioneered the Tent Methodists, a movement devoted to spreading the Gospel among the poor and oppressed, backing it up with some rudimentary education and medicine. His 'tents' were portable marquees, specially designed by himself and large enough to house 500–700 people. His was no small, one-man band. His team of preachers were soon covering much of the south-west. Grandfather George's missionary travels have a hint of those of W.G., fifty years later, when inexorably spreading cricket's good news with the United South of England Eleven.

W.G.'s irascible parting of the ways with Gloucestershire would likewise seem to have some correlation with Grandfather George's big bust-up eighty years earlier with Bristol's Wesleyans. He angrily resisted when they attempted a takeover of his whole operation, even though this meant expulsion from the Methodists' Society. Instead, determined to make his point, he upped his efforts and for a while turned the Tent Methodists into a national movement, for he was as cussed, when crossed, as W.G.

In all his activities Grandfather George would involve his family. At the height of his battle with the Wesleyans for example, his eldest sons wrote and circulated scurrilous, anonymous pamphlets. Instead of using a bell to call local colliery workers to tent meetings, he would drive around with his daughters, notably Bessie and Martha, singing 'The Songs of Zion' at the top of their voices.

W.G.'s legendary creativity in confounding both opponents and umpires clearly shows in the large number of Grandfather George's scholastic inventions, several of which he patented and marketed. With his son Ebenezer (an expert in Persian poetry) he invented an inflatable terrestrial globe that swelled like a huge balloon to an impressive 12 feet in circumference. If any symbol of Pocockian spirit was needed, there it was. The Pococks had taken on the world and made it theirs.

Martha was also caught up in another of her father's lifelong passions, the development of kite-flying. Experiments with pairs of large kites had encouraged George Pocock to believe that he could harness the wind to provide alternative means of transport to the horse. One experiment towards this possibility had involved Martha's brother Alfred, one year her junior, who was to become her children's devoted cricket coach. Alfred had volunteered to pilot a form of windborne sledge, on which he exuberantly travelled across the downs at vast speed before ending up in a stone quarry. Martha shared Alfred's boldness. When, in 1824, her father invented a chair-like device to be lifted by a 30-foot-wide kite, she sailed high into the air to become, at the age of twelve, the world's first 'aeropleust'. She also crossed the Avon gorge in a device that flew along a taut rope, though not, as the story often goes, soaring aloft, adrift like a hang-glider.

Grandfather George's experiments culminated in the pioneering of '*charvolants*' – four-wheeled vehicles propelled by a pair of kites that were patented as a form of 'car', a novel means of transport whose sightings on the roads of south-west England caused considerable surprise and alarm. It seems that these extraordinary machines really could carry people along at speeds of up to 30 mph, for in a recent BBC West television programme a Pocock charvolant was recreated from the original designs and taken to a beach at Weston-super-Mare. Although the four individual lines controlling the two kites were found to be 'fiendishly complicated', the test runs proved successful. 'George Pocock knew what he was doing,' commented the unscathed driver.

Pocock was not going to let the marriage of the doughty Martha, the first aeropleust, be a quiet affair. We can imagine the happy couple emerging from the west door of St Michael's, as the bells pealed forth from the fifteenth-century tower – they still do so occasionally today thanks to Bristol University's bell-ringing club – and the whole vast collection of Pococks gradually vacating the church and moving across to Prospect House for a noisy reception. But where were the Graces? However hard the Pococks looked for them, they were distinctly thin on the ground. The groom's mother Elizabeth was of course identifiable and looked encouragingly presentable. There was no sign of her husband, however. It was whispered that he was probably dead – and a thoroughly bad lot he had been, so rumour had it. As for the young groom, Dr Henry Grace, well, he seemed personable enough and smiled engagingly, even if he lacked a proper family. Word was that he had moved last year to the village of Downend to try to establish himself as a doctor – not an easy task. But what a helpmate he would find in Martha! That determined young lady could achieve anything she wanted. And with what passion she shared her young man's love of cricket.

* * *

Just into Somerset, two miles south of Bristol, we find Ashton Court, a stately home where both of W.G.'s paternal grandparents were in service. Owned since 1959 by Bristol City Council, it was for several centuries the home of one of Bristol's most prosperous merchant-venturer families, the Smyths, and it was in these grand surroundings that Henry and Elizabeth Grace, W.G.'s other set of grandparents, shared their early married life. It was not a happy union, however.

W.G.'s paternal grandmother, Elizabeth Mills, was a lady's maid who had moved to Ashton Court when her mistress had the misfortune to marry the philandering Sir Hugh Smyth. Elizabeth Mills herself soon afterwards married an unemployed footman, Henry Grace, and procured him a job with Sir Hugh, whose butler he eventually became. Grace however, proved an unreliable husband and the marriage was soon struggling. A description of him as 'a great coarse, potbellied unwieldy man, wholly deficient… in the Grace of God', though spoken in the course of a heated legal fracas, may not necessarily have been too far from the mark. At all events, Elizabeth Grace very soon left service at Ashton Court and in 1807 set up home in nearby Long Ashton village, renting No. 126 Long Ashton Road from the Smyths, a terraced house that survives today in private ownership. There, a year later, W.G.'s father Dr Henry was born.

By this time the two had gone their separate ways, Grace staying on in service at Ashton Court until his early death. W.G.'s grandmother meanwhile, converted her home into a small boarding school for young girls, calling it The Firs; the little school flourished. Elizabeth Grace and her two daughters were soon joined by a couple of teachers and an adjoining property (No. 128) was rented. By the time of her son's wedding at St Michael's, the former lady's maid had risen to prosperous middle-class status, and she was still running The Firs forty years on from its foundation, when W.G. was born.

W.G.'s father inherited his mother's industry. By twenty-two, a year before his marriage, he had become a licentiate in the Society of Apothecaries and a member of the Royal College of Surgeons and was ready to practise medicine. Before the Medical Act of 1858 it was possible for doctors to have no qualifications at all. Quacks abounded. It was each man for himself and it could take some years to build up a good practice. But as young Dr Henry began married life in Downend, he was nothing if not determined.

* * *

Downend House matched Henry's and Martha's ambitions. The yearly rent however, would have been well beyond them, so Dr Henry acquired and worked a small holding of 36 acres at nearby Beets Barton to help out. Whatever extra cash was needed, George Pocock would have supplied, delighted as he was that Martha had settled into her new life so earnestly. 'She was a cultivated lady,' wrote Brownlee, 'with an excellent musical touch and fond of country life. Gripping the fact that the success of a medical man is considerably affected by the tone and bearing of his wife, she entered heart and soul into the plans of her husband for the welfare of patients and the village generally'. W. G's *Memorial Biography* takes us a little further: 'W.G. bore a striking resemblance to her. She was a woman of magnificent physique and indomitable will.' That indomitable will was a huge help in the early years.

They were soon renting a half-acre field immediately behind the house, ideal for the doctor's horse and the family's pony and trap. Within a year or so, Dr Henry was galloping to and from the Coalpit Heath mines (owned by the Smyth family) as colliery surgeon, as well as Westerleigh, another village a few miles away to the north, where he was parish physician. A handsome man, with hair and side-whiskers in the manner of the Prince Consort, he relished his tough life. His practice eventually extended for a 12-mile radius around Downend and he had to cover considerable distances at all hours, but he never spared himself nor lost his high spirits, soon sustained by the pleasures of a young family and an equally young church up the road, whose strong evangelical credentials were entirely to Martha and Henry's taste.

W.G. was to inherit from his father his zest for the outdoor life. Dr Henry's happiest leisure hours in winter were spent riding to hounds and in the early summers he searched out whatever local games of cricket he could find, until, in 1841, encouraged by signs of considerable ability in his eldest son, the third Henry Grace in three generations, Dr Henry took the decisive step of forming his own club, The Mangotsfield. Home matches were played on the common at Rodway Hill, a mile across the fields from the village. 'Rodway Hill,' explained W.G. later, 'was the most convenient spot for the majority of the players, and, indeed, about the only place where ground could be had. It was common ground, but the members set to work with a will, and levelled and railed in about forty square yards.' Martha watched on in delight.

Among the many family friends who flocked to Downend House was Martha's younger brother Alfred, her fellow 'aeropleust', then in his late twenties and preparing to open his own lithographic business in Bristol. He was passionate about cricket and Dr Henry's chief lieutenant in the founding of the club. Indeed, the two brothers-in-law were to remain the team's stalwarts all its life. Alfred had carefully and successfully studied the game's skills. 'He made many good scores for the club,' wrote W.G., 'and his bowling won many a match.' Still a bachelor, based at Prospect Place, Alfred also created an occasional Pocock eleven, from three generations, letting it be known that they were 'ready to play any eleven bona fide of one family in England'.

From 1845 onwards, two young nephews of Martha's who happened to be outstanding cricketers, William Rees and George Henry Bayley Gilbert, spent seven consecutive summers staying with the Graces. George Gilbert had already played for Surrey and The Gentlemen, and their Pocock dynamism did much to transform The Mangotsfield's fortunes. They were adventurous spirits, whose futures lay on the other side of the world: both were later to play State cricket in Australia.

Their presence was crucial in The Mangotsfield's greatest early achievement, conquest of local rivals West Gloucestershire, a club four miles away at Coalpit Heath, run by Henry Hewitt, the bailiff of the largest of the local collieries, and his father, William, the senior representative of Sir John Smyth & Co., the principal employer in the district. Like the Graces, the Hewitts were devout Christians, their West Gloucestershire club having strong links with a new church they themselves had funded. In 1847, one year before W.G. was born, Dr Henry suddenly suggested a merger of the two teams. Henry Hewitt insisted that the name of West Gloucestershire be kept, but surprisingly agreed that Rodway Hill, four miles away from Coalpit Heath, should be the home base. Dr Henry must have been delighted. In addition to strengthening his side he had acquired a considerably more prestigious name. West Gloucestershire sounded much better than The Mangotsfield. Who knew? In the fullness of time, perhaps, there might even be a Grace-led Gloucestershire?

Disappointingly, the new combined team did not always carry all before them. Indeed, on one occasion, when without Rees and Gilbert, they were bowled out by Bath's Lansdown Club for just six. Dr Henry, sometimes an explosive character, was so furious at the deep humiliation that, although there was meant to be a second innings in the two-day fixture, he conceded the match there and then.

He was only a modest performer himself. 'A fair cricketer,' was W.G.'s telling summary. He showed little flair as a batsman, and it may be that Martha's outspoken detestation of left-handed batsmen had caused her husband (who bowled left-handed) to bat the wrong way round. Of one remembered occasion, when Dr Henry had opened the innings and carried his bat for a dour 17 in two hours, W.G. commented laconically, 'there was no tempting my father to hit'. His father's enthusiasm however, could not be faulted. He would anguish long and hard over the selection of his teams and, as fixtures against other clubs were necessarily very limited, he insisted on a practice match one evening every week. He also organised regular fielding practices. But, for all this, it would seem that W.G.'s cricket genes came more from the Pocock side of the family.

At Downend House Dr Henry and Alfred had soon fashioned a practice pitch for the eldest sons. ('Not much of a pitch; nor was it full size; but it was sufficient to teach the rudiments of the game'). W.G.'s books, confusingly stating it was 'on the lawn' and 'in front of the house', have led to the idea that it was situated on the front lawn. In fact, the practice wicket was created in a rented 1-acre field on the far side of the road, conveniently surrounded by a stone wall. The triangular plot, bounded by North Street, Carpenters Lane and Downend Road, is completely built over today.

But Downend House itself has survived the passing of nearly two centuries extremely well, even if some structural changes have seen the introduction of a central entrance, whereas, when Henry was galloping off and waving goodbye to Martha, the front door of the ivy-clad house was positioned to the right. The glass-fronted porch is a 1960s addition, reflecting the time it was bought by an engineering design firm. It currently houses an electronic publishing company.

Perhaps one day its importance as W.G.'s first home will be more properly reflected. It would be a wonderful home for a Grace Centre or Museum, combining the life and times of W.G. with insights into the life of a Victorian country doctor and his family.

2

An Uneven Start

Schooldays and early cricket, 1848–63

All the Graces were baptised in St James', Mangotsfield, for Downend's Christ Church had not yet acquired parish church status. St James' stood before a picturesque village green, and even though that green has now turned into shops and a parking space, the church still contrives to look special with its red-stone clock tower and gleaming, needle-sharp spire. Shimmering in the summer heat of 8 August 1848, as large quantities of Graces and Pococks clambered down from traps, barouches, coaches and carts, it offered a haven of cool peace.

It is a thirteenth-century church, but had been firmly modernised only shortly before the ceremony in that confident but slightly heavy mid-Victorian way. The font at the time was still situated at the back of the church, in the centre, and it was there that the family gathered as W.G. officially acquired those famous initials and the Revd Robert Brodie* did his best to calm the high-pitched cries of the future cricket champion, not best pleased that something like heavy rain seemed to be interrupting play.

One of the leading figures at the ceremony was the godfather, William Gilbert Rees, W.G.'s twenty-one-year-old cousin, whose dashing batting was currently enlivening Dr Henry's West Gloucestershire. With his bushy black hair, short beard and well-cut moustache, Rees looked a little older than his years. A former engineering student who was currently teaching, Rees nursed ambitions to make his fortune abroad. His adventurous nature had already won him a medal for bravery and he was a great favourite at Downend House. The new baby was to be given both his godfather's Christian names.

Little did the baby realise, as he basked in the fond gaze of his many admirers, that his future was already clearly mapped out by his parents. Just like his elder brothers, fifteen-year-old Henry, eight-year-old Alfred and seven-year-old Teddy, he would follow in father's footsteps and become a doctor. As for his leisure moments, he would devote himself to the manly game of cricket. For the moment, however, he could enjoy being the centre of attention, relaxing in his mother's ample arms. The wet weather seemed to be over. It would soon be time for play.

* * *

*   A family friend. When Mangotsfield's vicar retired, Dr Henry made the main speech at the presentation of a retirement present.

The Full Moon Hotel is in a somewhat neglected central part of Bristol, where the A38 leaves the St James Barton Roundabout for North Street. It was there, in 1854, that W.G., a rising six-year-old still attending a dame school in Downend, watched his first important match. The game had been arranged by his father after a meeting the previous winter at the Full Moon Hotel with William Clarke, the fifty-four-year-old manager and captain of the All-England Eleven. Clarke was a former bricklayer who had made a great success at Nottingham developing Trent Bridge as a cricket ground before the coming of the railways had encouraged him to start a travelling cricket circus, the All-England Eleven, featuring top professional players. The experiment thrived and All-England were soon playing thirty to forty fixtures each summer, more often than not 'against the odds' – teams of twenty-two or eighteen. Clarke was still a big draw himself. Although an accident meant he only had the use of one eye, in seven consecutive seasons he took well over two thousand wickets with his formidable underarm lobs. By the time of the discussions with Dr Henry, Clarke had already done much to popularise the game and All-England were to spawn several other important professional touring elevens.

The third participant at the meeting was the Full Moon's landlord, John Wintle, who was 'hoping to make a good speculation' and had offered Clarke the considerable sum of £65 to bring his team to Bristol (£45 of which would be pocketed by Clarke after he had paid his players £2 each). Dr Henry's part of the agreement was to provide twenty-two good local players from his West Gloucestershire club. The three-day match was to be played on 'Wintle's Field' at the back of the inn.

W.G. joined in the family excitement at preparations for the big match and was taken down several times to Wintle's Field to see the progress of the small team, led by his father's gardener, laying a special wicket. 'It was originally a ridge and furrow field,' recalled W.G. 'The pitch was first-rate, but the rest of the ground was rough and uneven.'

The Full Moon Hotel was a coaching inn that originally lay just outside the city, on the country road to Gloucester. Though Wintle's Field has been built over several times, the hotel today is currently doing brisk business as a backpackers' hostel, offering cheap 'dorm-style' accommodation to young people of all nationalities. It has become, according to its manager, 'an important fixture in Bristol's vibrant alternative nightlife and music scene'. This vibrancy certainly extends to its public bars that keep open till 2.00 and the stated lack of any 'early morning curfew'. The travel-hardened old pros of the All-England Eleven might have been mystified by the Full Moon's organic beers and food, and would certainly have struggled with a French commentary accompanying televised football, but could well have been tempted by the hotel's new 'shisha area' and the communal puffing on Turkish water-pipes.

The Full Moon in 1854 was already well over a hundred years old, and possessed 'a large yard and extensive stabling'. It had an attractive Dickensian feel, with its roaring open fires, plain wooden furniture and original carved oak staircase (all faithfully restored by the current owners), and was itself fairly 'vibrant'. Only a few years earlier, for example, the previous landlord had been fined for 'knowingly permitting and suffering people of notoriously bad character to assemble'. There had also been a fine for allowing people to drink 'during the hours of morning divine service', but Dr Henry was a man of the world, unfussed by petty niceties, pursuing his goals with determination.

The big match got under way at noon, when the umpires, both provided by the canny Clarke, came out to pitch the stumps. The bulkier umpire was pointed out at once to W.G., for it was Alfred Mynn, the former 'Lion of Kent', huge in stature as well as ability, weighing twenty stone when in his prime. W.G., sitting with his mother all day in her pony and trap, took it all in . . .

There was a big, steadily growing crowd and a real sense of occasion. Tents were dotted around the ground, one of which even housed a printing press that would 'chronicle the performances at the close of each day's play'. 'Numbers of jolly citizens' were sitting 'under tents – Turk-like – enjoying their pipes of peace and tankards of home brewed'. All-England, batting first, started very poorly, a reflection no doubt of the team's all-night journey from Leicestershire, but by three o'clock Wintle's Field was abuzz as George Parr and Julius Caesar were striking the ball firmly, and an exciting first day eventually ended with the West Gloucestershire Twenty-two slipping to 33 for 10 wickets in reply to All-England's 108. W.G. was disappointed that Uncle Alfred, opening for the twenty-two, had made only three, and his brother Henry, coming in first wicket down, an unlucky duck. Wintle's Field clearly favoured the bowlers. One West Gloucestershire batsman had had his thumb dislocated.

Next day began with another disappointment. Dr Henry, who had put himself among the tail-enders, the twentieth of the twenty-two batsmen, also failed to score and West Gloucestershire were all out for 43. There followed, however, the pleasure of watching fine hits by George Parr in All-England's productive second innings. There was much for Martha to explain as W.G. watched 'the Lion of the North', a handsome twenty-eight-year-old with fashionably full moustache and side-whiskers. Parr was ahead of his time in mixing defence with attack, had a unusual ability for turning the ball wristily to leg, and was startlingly speedy and acquisitive in his running between the wickets – all qualities for which W.G., as a young player, would himself be notable.

West Gloucestershire were clearly doomed, but for W.G. there was the pleasure of brother Henry's two wickets and Uncle Alfred's capture of Julius Caesar, one of the star batsmen of the era, to offset the disappointingly huge target of 239 that his father's side were set. On the final day Uncle Alfred (18) showed that Clarke's lobs could be countered by a careful, straight bat, and he was aided for a while by brother Henry (15). Wickets, however, tumbled fast, including Dr Henry's (bowled by Caffyn for 3). Clarke took 18 wickets in the match.

'I don't remember much about the cricket,' wrote W.G. years later, 'but I recollect that some of the England team wore top hats. My mother was very enthusiastic and watched every ball.' Alfred and Teddy were also spectators, having been given leave of absence from boarding school. When the successful fixture was repeated the next year, both were among the five family members in Dr Henry's West Gloucestershire team.

* * *

W.G. by this time was enjoying cricket in the garden of his parents' new Downend home, The Chesnuts (an idiosyncratic local spelling that several biographers have felt impelled to correct). 'My father, Henry and uncle,' wrote W.G., 'set to work early in 1851 and had a good wicket ready for the beginning of the cricket season.' The orchard was 'thickly studded with apple trees, a few of which had to be sacrificed'. Dr Henry and Uncle Alfred, with the experience of having coached three young Graces already, had real wisdom to impart when it came to the fourth. 'Have patience, my boy,' urged Dr Henry. 'Where there's a will, there's a way; and there is nothing you cannot attain if you only try hard enough.' 'Keep your left shoulder well forward,' admonished Uncle Alfred fiercely, 'and get over the ball! Until you do that you will never do any good! And keep your eye fixed on the bowler, and never lose sight of the ball from the time it leaves his hands! There must be no playing or hitting wildly!' During these happy practices even the family's dogs, we're told, obligingly acted as fielders in the deep. The ladies, too, took an interest: 'Rarely did we practise,' wrote W.G., 'without my mother being present as an onlooker' and, like her daughters, she 'fielded the ball when it came her way'. The sensibilities of the times demanded a description of ladylike daintiness. Martha and her daughters, however, were just as boisterous and noisy as the menfolk – as a young curate's wife, Blanche would be famous for tobogganing down the stairs on a tea-tray. Uncle Alfred's step-son, Billy Pocock, later recalled, 'All W.G.'s sisters were good cricketers. They could bat, bowl and field. His mother could also wield a bat with good effect.'

The Chesnuts, home to the Graces for thirty-five years, was knocked down in the late 1930s, but Brownlee has left us an eyewitness description: 'The Chesnuts was a square, plain building in those days, ivy creeping all over, with a pretty flower garden, and numerous outhouses. It stands on the main [Downend] road and walking up the carriage drive, past the lodge and old summer-house, you come to the main entrance. There's the large tulip tree in front, blooming and lighting up the place; beyond, the orchard, some 80 yards in length, a high wall on the left; Lady Cave Wood and the deep pool on the right; then away in the distance again, a fine stretch of fields, with the sun playing on the barley and oats, and you get a glimpse of Frenchay and Stapleton.'

If we walk along Downend Road from the ceramic mural of W.G. at the Willows Shopping Centre we will find, beside a lane called The Chestnuts, a red-brick telephone building, erected in the 1960s. It helpfully marks the far corner of The Chesnuts' frontage (a row of chestnut trees behind a high wall) that stretched halfway to the ceramic mural. The entrance to the carriage drive was at the Willows Centre end of the frontage, beside a lodge that served as Dr Henry's surgery. The house itself, with its back to Downend Road, was situated immediately behind the modern telephone building. The orchard stretched down and away from the modern lane.

We can recreate the Graces' garden better from the middle of the car-park at the back of the shopping centre, looking in the direction of the telephone building. In our imagination we are standing among apple trees. The Chesnuts is straight ahead, to the immediate right of the telephone building. To its right lie the end of the carriage driveway, a small flower garden and the practice pitch. 'We only had to step out of the house,' wrote W.G., 'and begin play.' Fifty yards behind us are the grounds of an adjoining property and a 'small piece of woodland, owned by the Cave family with several water-filled quarries'. As towering hits 'over long-on' were in danger of ending up in the quarries in Lady Cave's Wood, the wickets would have been pitched parallel to The Chesnuts, with the bowlers running in from our direction.

* * *

All the coaching and practice at The Chesnuts eventually led to W.G.'s first match for Dr Henry's team on Rodway Hill. West Gloucestershire were playing Bedminster, a club side from a village south of Bristol that Dr Henry would have known from his Long Ashton youth. W.G. was eight, rising nine.

To find the site of the ground where this match took place, we take a short five-minute walk from St James' Church down Rodway Hill Road. We ignore Manor Road on the right and the school on the left, continuing until the road curves left. There, at the beginning of the bend, through the trees on our immediate right, was once the entrance to the ground where, in 1857, the young W.G. played this first competitive game. Dr Henry was to vacate the ground, after twenty exhilarating years, in 1861, and, after being for a time part of a golf course, it has now reverted to wild common land. It was sited, so W.G. tells us, immediately above Mangotsfield Junction railway station. The station's ghostly remains are still visible today, hidden among trees and scrub on the course of the Bristol and Bath Railway Path.

W.G. acquitted himself satisfactorily in the match, if not exactly like a future champion, batting at number 11 and scoring 3 not out. There was plenty of family support, for, although William Rees and George Gilbert had emigrated to Australia to participate in the Victorian gold rush, W.G.'s father, uncle and three elder brothers were all playing; so, too, ten-year-old Billy Pocock, the stepson that Uncle Alfred had recently acquired from his late marriage to a middle-aged widow. Perhaps Bedminster had prior knowledge of the two young children selected by their opponents, for they arrived two men short. If so, they paid for their hubris. They lost heavily.

W.G. played two other matches that summer, both against Clifton, mustering one run from the two innings, and in the next few years his parents could have been forgiven for expressing disappointment that he looked less promising at this early age than any of his brothers. He was by now, moreover, at the first of two small boarding schools, chosen no doubt for taking cricket almost as seriously as religion.

Both schools have received scant coverage. Brownlee's bare comment that W.G. 'was entrusted to the care of Mr Curtis at Winterbourne' has been regularly repeated for well over a hundred years without the addition of anything more enlightening. We must visit Winterbourne Down, therefore, to find out a little more.

Though no longer a village, it is still an attractive residential area, high on a hill to the right of the old road to Gloucester, four miles beyond Downend. We find the site of W.G.'s old school at a recent housing development, Prospect Close, off old Dragon Road. At this turning, a straight and long carriage drive, at right angles to Dragon Road, led to a building a hundred yards away that W.G. knew well as Prospect House School.

Aaron Curtis, who ran the school, was a devout young widower, who early in life had founded, in other less spacious premises in Winterbourne, a small school of a dozen pupils with his mother as matron. How Dr Henry came to know of him is not clear, but as Winterbourne is very close to Coalpit Heath (where the West Gloucestershire club started) it may have been through the strongly evangelical Hewitt family. Aaron Curtis, who was connected with Winterbourne's Salem Methodist Church, could well have been recommended by the Hewitts. They would also have approved of Curtis' acquisition of a large tract of surrounding downs for his school's games.

W.G. joined the school in 1856 at the very moment that Aaron Curtis acquired his new premises, a large eighteenth-century building on the edge of Winterbourne Down, a former poorhouse, which he renamed Prospect House Academy. The name seems to have been both a tribute to the late George Pocock and a fitting comment on the school's position, lying well back from Dragon Road in its own grounds and overlooking sweeping countryside with the dark outline of the hills of Bristol on the distant horizon.*

* * *

In 1858, while W.G. was still a Prospect House pupil, the West Gloucestershire eleven had an exciting boost. W.G.'s thirty-one-year-old godfather, William Rees, had returned from Australia on a six-month mission to marry his childhood

---

* After Aaron Curtis' death, long after W.G. was there, Prospect House reverted to private use and was renamed Elmcroft, before finally being pulled down for the modern Prospect Close development.

sweetheart and win financial support for explorations of uncharted territories in New Zealand. The marriage took place in Worcester, and we may be sure all the Graces attended, for W.G.'s brother Henry was married there, too, in a joint ceremony. Both grooms were marrying their cousins. Henry's bride was Leeanna Pocock, and Rees was marrying Frances Gilbert, the sister of his cricketing friend George and the daughter of Martha's sister Rose. This confusing double union at Worcester was typical of the highly complicated intermarriage within the Grace-Pocock-Rees clan. It also created an early opportunity for the ten-year-old W.G. to get to know five-year-old Walter Raleigh Gilbert, Rose's son by her second marriage. Walter Gilbert was to become a fine Gloucestershire cricketer and feature most importantly in W.G.'s story.

Rees stayed a few weeks with the Graces at The Chesnuts that summer, enabling participation in at least three matches on bumpy Rodway Hill. 'His appearance was of great interest to me,' wrote W.G., 'and I watched his play most carefully. His old skill had not deserted him.' Rees, in his turn, was impressed by his godson and gave him every encouragement. 'After seeing my defence,' recalled W.G., 'he thought me such a promising young player that he presented me with a bat before he left. It had what I had long wished for, a cane handle.'

One of the matches in which they both participated became famous as the Battle of Rodway Hill. Dr Henry, just turned fifty, was still captaining his team with forty-five-year-old Uncle Alfred alongside. With Henry, Alfred and Teddy also in the team, West Gloucestershire had seven family members. Their opponents came from Redland Green, a village north-west of Bristol, close to Durdham Down. The Graces had turned up mid-morning to practise beforehand and 'had a fair number of spectators even at that early hour'. One of them, however, as W.G. recalled, 'had been drinking rather freely' and deliberately stretched himself out full-length, 'unpleasantly close to where we were playing', perhaps objecting to the roping off of a section of common by a privileged few. As the Redland team began to arrive, the irritated Dr Henry took decisive action. 'Calling up my brother Alfred, who had a fine reputation as a boxer, he ordered him to remove the obstinate individual.' The intruder rose and made something of a fight of it, but after two minutes of Alfred's flailing fists cried out 'Enough!' and fled across the common.

The two-innings match eventually got under way and wickets tumbled on both sides (W.G. making 2 out of the first innings total of 67). By late afternoon West Gloucestershire were batting again and 87-5 (with W.G. yet to go in), needing just 15 runs to win, when the objector re-appeared, this time with considerable reinforcements. 'It seemed absurd,' wrote Brownlee, 'that a cricket match should be delayed a second time for so small a matter; but there was no alternative. Alfred had a tough task this time; but, rising to the occasion, he polished off his opponent in an artistic and satisfactory manner.' It was only a temporary success. The objectors found a convenient pile of stones and began throwing them at West Gloucestershire. A free-for-all followed, with the Redland team supporting the Graces. We're not told whether W.G. joined in, but we can be sure that his spirited godfather, already a Queensland boxing champion, readily leapt in on seeing the objectors in the ascendant, and it is hard to believe that W.G. didn't follow him. Things evened up when the Graces resorted to the use of stumps and cricket bats as weapons, by which time Dr Henry 'had ridden off hurriedly to the nearest magistrate'. The fight was only ended by the magistrate's arrival and his threat of reading the Riot Act (which, though it had recently lost the death penalty, still could involve transportation abroad for life). That the match was then abandoned, when so close to a result, suggests that there had been real injuries.

Accounts make no mention of Martha, but she would rarely miss a match, and would have been there with W.G.'s only younger brother, six-year-old Fred, in her pony-and-trap. It might well have been her firm directive that had sent Dr Henry riding off for a magistrate. For W.G. it was another instructive experience. The Grace family, if crossed, gave no quarter.

In the next few years W.G. would play from June to August for his father's eleven and wherever his elder brothers' influence might get him a game with other Bristol clubs. He was still of slight build and very moderate height and his performances remained modest, apart from one fifty scored against Clifton in 1860 with the bat his godfather had given him. Indeed, the most remarkable feature of this period was not so much the cricket at all, but the all-pervasive influence of Uncle Alfred that saw W.G. travelling to some matches in a kite-powered '*charvolant*' shortly before the proliferation of telegraph wires and railway bridges put paid to the fond project for good. 'Beyond cricket we boys also went in for kite carriages', boasted W.G. years later, carelessly attributing the invention to Uncle Alfred. 'I may mention that we used to beat the carriages drawn by horses frequently, while on one occasion he [Uncle Alfred] raced and defeated the Duke of York's carriage on the London Road...'

* * *

W.G.'s extrovert sense of fun would not have made him a model student at a small boarding school. His preference for tough country pursuits over intellectual study would have soon surfaced. By 1860 he had joined Ridgeway House with younger brother Fred, a newly-opened establishment in a former mental asylum in Bristol's Upper Eastville district, about a mile away down Fishponds Road from Downend, run by the Revd Henry Malpas, whose two tutors included David Bernard, a twenty-year-old friend of Teddy's. A small man with spectacles, Bernard soon gave up teaching for medicine and later married W.G.'s sister Alice. As a Bristol doctor and a useful cricket all-rounder, well known to Brownlee, he was able to supply information about W.G.'s time at Ridgeway House (wrongly given as Rudgway by Brownlee and undergoing several other strange spellings subsequently). It seems a suspiciously rose-tinted view: 'W.G. earned the reputation of being a steady working lad, accurate at mathematics, with no mischief in him.' A further comment hints at a truer picture: 'He was passionately fond of collecting birds' eggs and snakes, which caused rather a division of feeling and opinion at The Chesnuts.' The snakes were 'the terror of his mother and sisters' and had to be smuggled into the house and hidden in secret corners. Scolding from Dr Henry was a regular consequence. Bernard, too, apparently supplied W.G. with confiscated marbles in return for his pupil putting in a good word on his behalf with sister Alice. W.G. duly became the school's marbles champion (an easier job than it sounds, for in 1861 there were only thirteen pupils in addition to the two Graces).

Ridgeway House disappeared some years ago to make way for the Redhill Drive and Close development, not far from the Upper Eastville intersection of the M32. Just to the north-east of today's small cemetery, it stood in large grounds in essentially a country setting, with the River Frome nearby.

* * *

In the Ridgeway years W.G. began to feature a little as a bowler, but it was not until his fifteenth year, in 1863, that he made positive progress. There was a good reason for this. Suddenly he could play over twice as many games of cricket, for his parents had removed him from school altogether and found him a tutor.

John Walter Dann was not the most obvious choice at barely twenty, but he was an engaging Irishman with a degree from Dublin and a protégé of the Graces under whose patronage he would take up holy orders and become a long-serving curate and vicar at Christ Church. Like another protégé, David Bernard, Dann would also marry one of W.G.'s sisters (the lively Blanche) and though less of a cricketer than Bernard, he was nonetheless absolutely devoted to the game. Indeed, W.G.'s ability to translate the *Gallic Wars* was not at all enhanced by the ease with which he could get his tutor onto the subject of Surrey's Julius Caesar. Yet Dann's tutoring and genial advice helped a new maturity of outlook. W.G. slowly began to temper fiery enthusiasm with some canniness.

The year began alarmingly with a bout of pneumonia that might have killed him. On his recovery, he began to show that not all of Uncle Alfred's remonstrations had been in vain, with 86 for his father's eleven against Clifton on Durdham Down; 74 for Frenchay on their (still delightful) village green; and 15 Clifton College wickets for brother Henry's eleven. He also scored a 50 for Dr Henry's latest creation, the Gentlemen of Gloucestershire (an occasional, family-centred team) in their match against the Gentlemen of Somerset. There were, of course, some setbacks. Teddy at that time played regularly for Lansdown (sometimes walking the 10 miles to Bath and back, if father had the horses and mother the pony-and-trap) and that year W.G., when playing against Lansdown for Clifton, not only had the agony of getting a pair but also of being out both times to Teddy. There was another pair, too, at Bath, when he was playing for a Lansdown twenty-two against George Parr's All-England Eleven – a failure slightly offset by Teddy's blistering 74, struck with such authority that Parr invited him to join his forthcoming winter tour to Australia and New Zealand. Teddy's initials of E.M. were now becoming famous.

When, a little later, the All-England Eleven came to Durdham Down to play Twenty-two of Bristol and District, W.G. made amends with a meritorious 32 despite the hostility of 'Tear 'em' Tarrant and the even faster Jackson, the best professional bowlers in England. The lobs of Cris Tinley in the style of William Clarke proved his undoing: 'Tinley's first over I played carefully; in the second I decided to hit, and hit him into the scoring-tent. The hit was loudly cheered; I was pleased, felt elated, got over-confident, and paid the penalty. In my haste to repeat the stroke, I ran out too far in the third over, missed the ball altogether, and was clean bowled.' It was not the act of a potential champion, and there were critical words from his parents and Uncle Alfred. John Dann's more tempered advice would have been invaluable.

Parental frustrations were understandable. Like his brothers, W.G. had enjoyed a very special cricketing education: early opportunities to watch the country's best players; a good practice wicket; schools which took the game seriously; and a family-run club allowing participation in adult cricket. A decent return in runs and wickets was expected after all that support. Young William Gilbert was hardly cutting the mustard. The next winter, however, W.G. suddenly began to grow so fast that he was soon not only the tallest member of his family but an impressive six foot one. The effect on his cricket was to be significant.

3

An Acquisitive Spirit

The emerging star, 1864–66

Down on Bristol's Spike Island we find one of the city's outstanding attractions, Brunel's original steamship, the *Great Britain*, painstakingly restored and most imaginatively displayed in the Great Western Dockyard, where she had been built. Every effort has been made to transport visitors into the middle of the nineteenth century. We wander down passages, peer into kitchens and cabins and are greeted by 'authentic' sounds and smells. We are back in time. So, as we stand on the windswept deck of the world's first great ocean liner, dwarfed by its single funnel and three towering masts, the figure of Teddy easily materialises, waving gaily down to W.G. and the rest of the family. The much-acclaimed E.M. was setting out on the *Great Britain* with the other eleven members of George Parr's touring team of 1863–64 on the long voyage to Australia.

He was to be well paid for his six-month absence from England, happily pocketing £250 like the rest of the all-professional team, despite his exclusive amateur status. Brunel's glorious ship not only exemplifies the Victorians at their most resourceful but also reminds us of the acquisitive spirit of the Graces, so in tune with the strong nineteenth-century ethic of personal advancement in the national and imperial interest. When opportunities arose, the Graces seized them eagerly. An acquisitive culture meant never underselling oneself; aiming at new excellence; achieving the very best of all possible outcomes.

E.M. pioneered the way for W.G. Only the previous year, for example, M.C.C. had stretched their rules to pick him, a twenty-year-old non-member, for an important game at Canterbury. E.M. responded by scoring a century. But a century wasn't enough. He smashed 192 not out. But that, too, wasn't enough. So he took all ten Kent wickets in a single innings and in one rollicking game established himself as England's finest all-rounder. As we wander around the *Great Britain* in the steps of E.M., we can better understand the inspiration W.G. received from his famous elder brother and how, from the ages of sixteen to eighteen, he elevated himself, almost unthinkably, into actual rivalry with him, as the boy of 1864 who 'promises to be a good bat' and 'bowls very fairly' changed into the 'magnificent batsman' of 1866, 'with defensive and hitting powers second to none'.

E.M.'s courageous and acquisitive spirit matched that of the godfather W.G. so much admired, William Gilbert Rees, and when Parr's tourists crossed from

Australia to New Zealand, E.M. had been able to arrange a meeting and catch up with his adventures. Taking his young wife with him on his explorations in New Zealand, Rees had driven three thousand sheep across many miles of uncharted and difficult territory before becoming one of the first settlers to reach Lake Wakatipu in central Otago, where he founded Queenstown, establishing himself in a holding of some 300,000 acres. When his base was invaded during the Otago gold-rush, Rees embraced the challenge, helping the wild prospectors by ferrying their gold to safety in his whaleboats and bringing them back life-saving provisions. 'He would turn out in the dead of night,' recalls his biographer, 'with a revolver tucked in his belt, to ensure that every hungry miner had a share of flour and food when his ferry-boat docked.' When a brawny miner chose to argue, Rees 'drew on his boxing skills and felled his aggressive critic with a single blow'. At the height of the gold rush he was working as a carrier, coach proprietor, lighter-man, boat-builder, hotel-keeper, store-keeper, contractor, sawyer, gold-buyer, slaughter-man, baker, land agent and run-holder. But for all his entrepreneurial expertise he never forgot his Pocock background, also helping build a church where he became a popular lay reader and, in the spirit of muscular Christianity, he always thirsted for sport. His imaginative attempts to stretch the rules of cricket, like those of his godson, became legendary. In one upcountry match he refused to leave the crease on being bowled. He couldn't possibly be given out, he declared. His wicket might indeed be broken, but there was a reason for this. He had been most unfortunately distracted by a flock of sheep on a distant hill . . . The two W.G.s had much in common.

Today Rees' Queenstown is a flourishing tourist centre, advertising itself most appropriately as 'the outdoor adventure capital of the world'. Just as Bristol has many reminders of the godson, so, too, Queenstown abounds with tributes to the godfather. Eichardt's Hotel, for example, proudly acknowledges that it was once Rees' wool store before its conversion at the time of the gold rush. There is also a Rees Bridge, a Rees Hotel, a Rees River, and, near the pier on Rees Street, a larger-than-life bronze statue depicting W.G.'s godfather, handsomely bearded and resolute, with his overcoat flapping in a howling wind and a magnificently horned merino ram nestling beside him. It is the work of sculptor Minhal Al Halabi. 'William Rees was a talented artist,' he comments, 'and I based the face of the sculpture on a self-portrait of his – William in his prime, and as he saw himself.' The characteristics that Minhal sought to bring out sound very much like those of his godson. 'He was a strong, determined character, with a real physical presence about him. If he entered a room, people took notice. He had the chest of a swimmer and the hands of a boxer.' W.G. was to exchange regular letters with his godfather for forty years. There was a deep respect between the two. Queenstown's fine statue honours one of the most important influences in W.G.'s life.

* * *

In 1864, at the age of sixteen, W.G. achieved 1,000 runs and 100 wickets from his many club matches. The most important of these occurred in a tour he undertook with South Wales, an opportunity that had arisen from the Graces' extensive social network. Two rich acquaintances of Dr Henry, Sir John Talbot Dillwyn-Llewellyn Bart. and Captain Samuel George Homfray, whose families ran prosperous ironworks in south Wales, had established a nomadic team emulating the newly founded I Zingari and Free Foresters in fostering the ethos of gentlemanly cricket. They favoured upper-class opponents in England with country estates, and had formed a strong relationship with the hierarchies at Lord's and The Oval. There were early fixtures, too, at Bristol, where Dr Henry and Uncle Alfred were their contacts and sometimes played for South Wales. W.G.'s elder brothers had also participated in the club's annual excursions to London. For the first match of their latest tour, funded by Captain Homfray, Alfred was unavailable, but Henry and Teddy had both been asked to play. When it became clear that E.M's late return from Australia was a problem, Dr Henry persuaded Homfray to take W.G. instead.

The first match was at The Oval, where W.G. opened the South Wales bowling with brother Henry against a team of Surrey amateurs. At the highly impressive modern cricket facility that is today's Oval, it is hard to envisage the ground that W.G. visited in 1864, converted into cricketing use from a market garden only twenty years earlier. Its pavilion was very new, a wide, one-storey structure, offering members a long clubroom with changing-rooms behind. It was elevated on a grassy bank, providing a good view for those members lucky enough to find a seat under its front colonnade of seven arches. The adjacent eighteenth-century tavern and entrance gave the ground a pleasing sense of antiquity. The familiar buildings of today were singularly lacking, except for some gasometers outside and St Mark's Church, of whose tower W.G. had a fine view as he stood and watched the bowlers going back to their mark at the pavilion end.

The Oval's reputation had been made by the brilliant Surrey teams of the 1850s, but W.G. was not in the slightest overawed. He took 4-59 in his twenty-six four-ball overs, delivered at medium-fast in the round-arm action that had finally been legalised only that year. He impressed, too, with his batting. Though in his first innings he was defeated early on by one of John Walker's skilful lobs, in the second he reached 38, he and Henry putting on the highest stand of the innings. So when the South Wales captain John Lloyd announced that for the next fixture of the tour, down at Brighton, W.G. would be dropped for a stronger player, there was considerable outrage in the Grace camp. Henry, about to return to his Bristol medical practice, let fly. If his young brother were not selected, that would be the end of the Grace connection with South Wales! W.G. was hurriedly re-selected.

The country doctor's son would have been impressed by his first sight of Brighton, still aglow in the aftermath of its Regency embellishments. He could not but marvel at the oriental fantasy that was the Royal Pavilion; the startling Gothic Revival of St Peter's Church; and the sheer excitement of the Royal Suspension

Chain Pier. The sea-facing squares and crescents, expressions of a grandiose architectural ambition, still had a wonderful freshness about them. The West Pier was currently under construction and the Grand Hotel would open in a week's time.

South Wales were meeting the Gentlemen of Sussex at the Royal Brunswick Ground, which faced directly onto the seafront, close to the modern boundary between Brighton and Hove, but would soon fall victim to the need to house the burgeoning middle classes. Today its site is covered by the twentieth-century apartment blocks of Third and Fourth Avenues.

It was a large ground, run by a brewery whose wares were advertised over the main seafront entrance ('Vallance & Catt: fine ales and foreign spirits'). The brewery hired excellent cricket managers, like the famous old Sussex wicket-keeper Tom Box, and this, in turn, had led to a good wicket, regularly used by the Sussex County Club before its move to nearby Eaton Road. The ground was enclosed by a fence; open fields lay either side; and the Brunswick Cricket Ground Hotel, run by the same brewery, was close by, facing out to sea.

South Wales chose to bat, and W.G., first wicket down, was soon joining his captain John Lloyd, an accomplished all-round sportsman whose family held large estates in Breconshire. Lloyd was surprised to find himself outpaced by a boy half his age, as the two of them participated in a stand of 188. His confident young partner seemed at ease with everything: sand would blow across the pitch but he brushed it off with diligence and equanimity; the gulls might swoop and cry, but he took no notice; the sea made its steady and soporific protests against the shingle, but he kept alert; fishing boats with their tall masts put out to sea and later returned, but he hardly seemed to notice; ships idled mysteriously on the distant horizon but the boy only had eyes for the Gentlemen's latest field changes. He was, indeed, a revelation. He might look and sound like a young village yokel, but he batted with all the skill of the best-trained gentleman.

Though Lloyd was out for 82, W.G. was not going to call it a day just because he had scored a century and there were jugs of Vallance & Catt's best ale already being consumed in the pavilion. 'When associations and surroundings are favourable,' he later wrote of this innings, 'there can be little doubt that perseverance will work wonders.' He was cross with himself when he finally fell on the second day for 170. A double century was in prospect. Maybe even more. To give away his wicket when well set was an irritation, and it took time that evening to be at ease with his team's high spirits at the Royal Brunswick. But Captain Samuel Homfray, who batted down the order and only really came into his own in the evenings, soon started on his outstanding repertoire of saucy music hall songs. They became a very jolly company, and W.G. began to appreciate the further pleasures that cricket had in store, beyond the hours of play . . .

On the final day by the sea, the Sussex Gentlemen, following on, batted long enough to save the match, but there was still time for W.G., in his 56 not out, to show South Wales that he played much straighter than the norm, defended with more resolution, hit with greater wisdom and timed the ball with extra sweetness. As for Brighton, it was the first of many British holiday resorts that he would return to with undiminished enthusiasm year after year.

* * *

A week later – Homfray's tours were leisurely affairs – W.G. scored a 50 on his first appearance at Lord's, playing alongside E.M., newly returned from Australia. Their opponents, M.C.C., contained at least one Viscount, Marquis and Earl, a good smattering of University Blues, plus a single professional, Tom Hearne, who did half the bowling. Lord's was more impressive in its high-class clientele in the 1860s than in its pitches and facilities, which to a newcomer would have been distinctly disappointing.

W.G. and E.M. returned to Lord's a week later for South Wales' second match there, against I Zingari, opening the innings together. W.G. made a well-considered 34 and Teddy a fiery 55. W.G. top-scored in the second innings with 47, helpfully impressing influential I Zingari personalities like Sir Spencer Ponsonby and Robert Fitzgerald, the recently appointed M.C.C. secretary. Similarly, in the last two matches of the South Wales tour – versus Knickerbockers at the Cattle Market Ground, Islington, and at Southgate – W.G. enjoyed further forays into London society. Coping with the worst of the snobbery and learning to play the system were skills he needed to acquire.

Though the Brighton century was the most spectacular of W.G.'s successes on the six-match tour, the impression he made on M.C.C.'s secretary at Lord's probably proved more important. He had never met anyone quite like 'Bob' Fitzgerald before. If Lord Harris was in awe of 'the magnificence of his swagger, the luxuriance of his beard, the fun that rolled out of him so easily and the power of his swiping', the flamboyant Fitzgerald must have been startling to the young W.G. But each impressed the other. Only three years later Fitzgerald would further W.G.'s career (and at the same time consolidate the club's future) by putting him up for M.C.C. membership. Both his social background and his age were against him, but, proposed by the Treasurer and seconded by the Secretary, he would be duly elected.

* * *

In 1865 W.G. made his debut in first-class cricket, for the Gentlemen against the Players at The Oval, standing in as E.M.'s last-minute substitute, and success there as a bowler led to three further important games for sides of Gentlemen. But although he showed in all of them that he could compete on equal terms with the best players in the country, he was mainly occupied that season and the next in minor matches in the Bristol area. He demonstrated his exceptional class by gaining well over 2,000 runs and 200 wickets in both years.

We are stopping in the middle of that second summer to meet W.G. at one such minor fixture, on the brink of both his eighteenth birthday and the two matches at The Oval that would really make his name. We are a few miles north of Bristol, at Knole Park, outside Almondsbury, close to the intersection of the M4 and M5 and we have been drawn here by a famous West Gloucestershire team photograph, featuring eight family members, that was taken at Knole Park in July 1866.

Dr Henry's team is seated in front of the trunk of a huge tree, with a couple of marquees and part of the Knole Park cricket field behind them. The slim W.G. is difficult to recognise, with his thin moustache and straggling side-whiskers meeting under the chin. He seems a minor presence compared to his three elder brothers beside him, all sporting heavy, dark mutton chops: Henry in top hat and striped shirt, looking quaintly old-fashioned; E.M. with arms folded, relaxed and confident; Alfred, the Rodway Hill pugilist, hunched up, bearded and half-hidden by Fred, a short, stocky and pugnacious fifteen-year-old. Uncle Alfred is there, of course, in his whites, clearly still active at fifty-three, even if the heavy beard is greying; and the final family team member is his tough-looking young step-son, Billy. Dr Henry sits at the back of the team in his carefully buttoned suit and tall top hat, aloofly ignoring the camera and looking much younger than his fifty-eight years, not a grey hair visible in his moustache and side-whiskers.

There is something vaguely unsettling about the photograph. Of course, the exposure time was so long in the 1860s that stony faces were normal, but, even so, these country house cricketers look more like embattled soldiers resting in a war zone. For all the sedentary poses, they look intensely acquisitive.

Accounts of the match, however, suggest that the young Graces had all been on their best behaviour, something their parents would have insisted upon, for staying two or three nights at Knole Park had become an annual treat, not to be prejudiced by tearaway tendencies. Knole Park was a lovely little ground, high up on a hill overlooking the village of Almondsbury, on the country estate of fifty-year-old Colonel Thomas Chester Master, whose castle-like home, complete with octagonal sixteenth-century tower, had picture-book views over the Bristol Channel. The Colonel was captaining an eleven which included his son and heir, the local vicar and forty-year-old Sir Charles Cuyler, Bart. The Masters were a military family of excellent pedigree and there were useful contacts for Dr Henry and Martha to cultivate. Colonel Master's elderly father had been Gentleman Usher to King George IV, William IV and Queen Victoria.

In a warm-up match at Knole Park the day before this fixture, W.G. had led the scoring to clinch Bedminster's victory, with Teddy and Fred in support. Now, on the first day of the West Gloucestershire match, it was Teddy who led the West Gloucestershire charge to 196 and he followed this up by skittling out most of Knole Park before the close. The aggression beneath the surface of the photograph was exemplified in the field, where, with the exception of elder brother Henry, the Graces flung themselves around with passion, exuding anguish at any run conceded. There were long recriminations when, as reported by the *Bristol Mercury*, W.G.'s brother Alfred inadvertently caused a small set-back: 'An unmistakable "sitter" in the long-field would have been secured by Gilbert Grace had not his brother, A. Grace, run out and caused a collision during which the ball dropped through.'

Dr Henry surely said a thing or two about refinement that evening, for the next day there was distinctly less belligerence on display, and the Knole Park tail briefly wagged. 'Colonel Master was in good form,' noted a surprised reporter, 'hitting E.M. about very freely despite the destructive nature of his "roundhanders" the previous night.' Brother Henry, who, as the calmest of the volatile fraternity, had been made captain, refused to let Teddy and Gilbert open the bowling when Knole Park followed on, and he and Uncle Alfred allowed the home team to make some encouraging hits. However, even with the addition of some generous wides from the West Gloucestershire skipper, the home team still lost by an innings.

The Knole Park cricket 'week' was essentially a big social occasion, attracting all the local gentry. 'The weather being beautifully fine,' noted the *Bristol Mercury*, 'large and fashionable assemblages have visited the charming grounds of Colonel Master'. The upper-class ambience was further useful experience for the rough-edged younger Graces. Dr Henry and Martha knew exactly what they were about.

There is not much evidence today of the Chester-Masters at Knole Park. The family eventually sold the country seat and in the 1930s it became an 'exclusive enclave of period homes'. The imposing house was demolished in 1970. The lodge house remains, in altered form, together with the sixteenth-century octagonal tower of the old mansion, which escaped the bulldozers by being shortened and affixed to a modern property. A splendid old cedar tree nearby, standing on a small green, raises our hopes that this indeed may be the very one under which Dr Henry's West Gloucestershire once posed so menacingly.

* * *

W.G. went to The Oval for the first of his two career-changing innings that August after making 91 and 87 for Stapleton on bumpy Durdham Down. His invitation to play for England against Surrey at The Oval, one of the most popular matches of the season, had come from Vyell Edward Walker, an influential Surrey Committee member and one of seven famous cricketing brothers from Southgate. Teddy (or 'V.E.') Walker, a fine straight-driving hitter and a leading lob bowler, would himself be captaining England.

Play began at 12.10 p.m. with a stop for lunch at 3.00. England batted first, and at 1.30 p.m., with the score at 90-3, W.G. joined the experienced Sussex professional Charlie Payne. Ninety minutes later, as they made their way across to the Oval Tavern for lunch, they were 203-3, with a beaming W.G. 72 not out. He had not made a first-class 50 before, and, like all those who scored 50s at The Oval, he would be receiving a bat from the Surrey Committee.

The second session of the day was another long one, ending at 7.00 p.m. W.G. enjoyed himself, driving one full-toss 'with tremendous vigour to the entrance gate for

5' and making 'two huge drives for 5, one past the tree'. There were no boundaries. Everything had to be run, apart from any unlikely hits that went right out of the ground, but W.G. was an enthusiastic runner, who had taken to competing at amateur athletic events, and there was no question of surrendering his wicket through tiredness. By the time stumps were drawn England were 444-8 and he was 187 not out.

It was cold and wet the next morning. They eventually started at 1.55 p.m. and by the time they stopped early for lunch, when further rain fell at 2.40 p.m., he had taken his score to 217. It was already by far the highest score made at The Oval, eclipsing the best effort of Surrey's own Harry Jupp. Play did not resume till 4.00 p.m. but W.G.'s concentration remained resolute. When England were finally bowled out for 521, he was undefeated on 224. He had batted, on and off, for nearly six hours. If the bowlers over-pitched, he drove them straight and over the top; if short, he pulled 'with unerring precision to broad field or square-leg'. The fieldsmen were constantly moved around, sometimes mid-over, but he continued to place the ball carefully between them. He scored 92 of his 224 in singles.

We get an insight into the confident attitude W.G. brought with him to this important match from what happened on the third day (when Surrey sank to a heavy innings defeat). W.G. was absent. Instead of pressing home the advantage with his team-mates, W.G. had opted to compete in an athletics meeting at the Crystal Palace. His success there duly became part of his legend. A double century one day and victory in the 440 yards hurdles the next. What athleticism! What pertinacity! W.G. did not let on that he had actually been a little less than totally successful at the Palace, having blown up in the quarter-mile and been left behind in the two sprints. Nor do his biographers even hint of the arrogance of youth that underpinned the absenteeism.

* * *

The cricket in between the two important matches at The Oval was the usual strange mixture of the major and minor. There was also rivalry with E.M. at the West of England Athletics Festival at the Clifton Zoological Gardens which ended in much bad feeling when W.G., who had never beaten E.M. over 100 yards, did so by stealing two yards unfairly at the start. ('There was family coolness for a bit,' conceded Brownlee gently.)

One minor match was of particular significance, even though W.G. failed twice in it with the bat. It took place in Middlesex. He and E.M. had been included in the United South of England's Eleven to play John Walker's Fifteen of Southgate.

* * *

John Walker was the eldest of the seven Walker brothers who had all learned their cricket at Harrow and Cambridge. He had founded the Southgate club, developed a fine wicket and made it a ground of importance with invitations to M.C.C., the All-England Eleven and many other strong and influential clubs (including South Wales). Crowds of up to 10,000 would attend the biggest matches. Railway companies ran special trains on such days to Colney Hatch Station, bringing spectators to the ground on the fringes of the Walkers' large country estate, whose 300 acres stretched over what was to become suburban New Southgate and Palmer's Green.

The beautifully unspoilt Southgate cricket field is worth a visit, for it still retains close resonances with W.G. Most appropriately, it is known today as The Walker Ground, and it has such a fine square that it has hosted many Middlesex county matches in modern times. The Southgate Cricket Club fields four teams in various Middlesex leagues, and, proud of their heritage, the members display in their pavilion a bat that once belonged to John Walker himself.

We can also visit the Walkers' actual home, Arno's Grove, a large house on busy Cannon Hill which currently serves as the Southgate Beaumont Nursing Care Centre and has a blue plaque commemorating the brothers. It is not quite as it was when the Graces stayed there. After its sale in 1928 to the North Metropolitan Electricity Company, extra office blocks were built and the mansion was faced in red brick.

There is a second building at Southgate that W.G. knew well. On the other side of Waterfall Road, overlooking the ground and lending it distinction, is Christ Church, designed by George Gilbert Scott and boasting pre-Raphaelite windows with designs by Morris, Burne-Jones and Rossetti. Its construction was funded by the Walkers, who were deeply committed Christians, one of their brothers-in-law serving as its first vicar. At the time of W.G.'s visit in 1866, its stonework was brand-new, its tower and spire brighter and even more eye-catching than today. A hundred and fifty years on, a family vault marks the Walkers' last resting-place.

While at Southgate we should reflect on the oddity of W.G. and E.M. playing for the United South of England Eleven. This all-professional touring team had been founded only the year before. How could two young men be participating in such an overtly money-making venture without besmirching their amateur credentials? Apparently, however, the amateur-professional distinction was not such a touchy subject in the 1860s as it was soon to become. The seeds of the fixture had been sown at the end of the previous season, when E.M. and Isaac Donnithorne Walker had played together against the United South at The Oval for the Gentlemen of Surrey, and the Walkers were sufficiently taken with the idea of this new southern-based professional eleven to give it the encouragement of the fixture at Southgate. To help draw in the crowds, the Walkers were more than happy at E.M.'s suggestion that two of the most exciting young prospects in English cricket should boost the United South. And if the two Graces cared to demand liberal expenses, that would be entirely up to them.

Martha and Dr Henry would not have missed the opportunity of staying with their sons at Arno's Grove with its heady mix of evangelical faith, philanthropy and a prosperous family brewery. There was much inspiration for their own endeavours to be found at Southgate. The Walkers had not only created their own powerful club, but, in the late 1850s, had started a Middlesex side which by 1866 had just become the official County Club, one that they were now running and would continue to run, as a family, for several decades, providing not just the captains but also many of the officials . . .

* * *

In his second career-making match at The Oval, in late August 1866, W.G. represented the Gentlemen of the South (who included the youngest of the Walkers, Isaac Donnithorne, an outstanding batsman) against the Players of the South. The Players, ironically, contained many of W.G.'s recent United South teammates, including its prime-movers, both fine left-handed bowlers, Edgar Willsher and Jim Lillywhite. Despite the quality of the attack, W.G. gave no chances as he scored an undefeated 173. The Players encountered stroke-play of unusual power. One 'grand drive' past Willsher 'reached the far end of the ground' while 5 were run; a straight drive off Lillywhite 'reached the very extreme end of the ground, for which they ran 6'. W.G. pounded both sides of the wicket with equal force, lifting another Lillywhite delivery 'over the heads of the fielders on the on-side for another 6, which 'brought down the house'.

He was only eighteen, but in his eight first-class matches of 1866 he had averaged over 50 and taken a useful clutch of wickets. Comparisons were already being made with Alfred Mynn, and one enthusiast emotionally presented him with a pair of yellowing pads. They had been used, he explained, by the great Mynn. W.G. alone was worthy to wear them.

Henry and Martha were filled with understandable pride. It had been an impressively swift metamorphosis. The son who had begun so inauspiciously and had seemed something of an ugly duckling was now a very fine swan indeed. Their pride was tempered, however, by the slightest wisp of anxiety. Was their darling Gilbert perhaps becoming just a little too full of himself?

4

A County of Graces

Dr Henry's swansong, 1867–71

The Downend ceramic mural, showing W.G. sitting padded up with his back to The Chesnuts, is particularly appropriate to the one-sided battle of wills that was going on in the late 1860s between W.G. and his father. Dr Henry was urging him to attend medical school and work seriously as his apprentice. But W.G. wasn't keen. His cricket was going too well in the summers, and there were plenty of other diversions in the winter months – country sports that kept him fit and amused.

Dr Henry's worries were compounded by the influence Gilbert was having on his youngest son, Fred. Both lads were far too high-spirited for their own good, and things had got even worse since their blossoming friendship with Billy Pocock, who was similarly empty-headed about the future and for ever hanging around the cricket net at The Chesnuts. All three could sometimes be tearaways, a real embarrassment.

Criticism of Gilbert was proving, of course, the more difficult the more success he enjoyed with his cricket. After a modest season in 1867 he had brilliantly topped the country's averages the next year with a remarkable 65.33 from his seven first-class matches. Among three important centuries had been the triumph of 134 not out for the Gentlemen versus Players at Lord's, the biggest game of the season. No-one in the long history of the fixture had ever scored so many for the Gentlemen. Then in 1869 had come his election to M.C.C. membership, with all the major matches and extra successes that this opened up. After his six centuries and 1,320 runs in 1868, backed up by 73 wickets, people were saying that he was the country's new champion. Henry and Martha were thrilled to read in *Lillywhite's Companion* that their Gilbert was 'generally admitted to be the most wonderful cricketer that ever handled a bat. A certain scorer off any bowling and the quickest run-getter in England'.

But away from the cricket there was no encouragement at all. Dr Henry had found Gilbert a liability as an apprentice, a young fool happy to give his patients entirely the wrong medicine, regardless of consequences. Similarly, his attendance at the Bristol Medical School had been minimal. It didn't help, of course, that his mother so doted on him. Provided her Gilbert kept scoring bags of runs, she didn't seem to care. Indeed, her scrapbooks of his every innings seemed to be getting obsessive . . .

Dr Henry was right to be anxious. Some cheerful reminiscences by Billy Pocock late in life give an idea of the Chesnuts' atmosphere at around this time. One story concerned a local cricket tour that he had undertaken with W.G. and Fred in a hired caravan:

> We came to a toll gate at twelve o'clock at night. It was closed so we called the old toll man up who opened the gate and demanded payment. There was, inevitably, a bit of an argument over this and I suppose we got rather noisy, for suddenly his wife, a peevish old dame, appeared at a window, asking what we were doing. She had a farthing candle in her hand, and W.G., who was a brilliant shot, hurled an apple with all his considerable strength and scored an absolute bull's-eye on the candle. The old lady screamed and fell back into the room; the toll man rushed indoors; and we rushed off, delighted and amused that we'd got through free. Next day we were playing a match some twelve miles further on, and had just sat down to lunch when, to our dismay, there was the old toll man, who'd walked the twelve miles, threatening to have us locked up. W.G., however, paid him off with half a sovereign.*

Another reminiscence began with the three lunching at The Chesnuts after a hard morning's cricket practice, when the parlour-maid came in, announcing that 'there's a big man here who seems to be in pain and wants to see the doctor'. So they hastened to Dr Henry's surgery, where they found a collier suffering from toothache. 'Don't worry,' said Fred. 'My brother will fix things. Come here, my man.' And he sat him down in a chair. W.G. protested quietly that he had never drawn a tooth in his life, but they found him a pair of forceps and pushed him forward:

> First, we took precautions – Fred sat on the patient's feet, I sat on his head. W.G., who had wrists like iron, gave a mighty pull. The man rose with a howl, throwing me against the wall and nearly sending Fred through the window. He rushed out of the house, holding his jaw, calling out, 'That big fellow has lifted the top of my head off!' We returned to the net. All was fine for a while. Dr Grace, returning late afternoon, came out into the garden, enjoying a cigar and was enquiring about our practice when the maid came in with the news that a man 'with a swollen head' was asking for him in the surgery. We crept back and peered through the window. The man's jaw was in a fearful state. 'Who's been butchering you like this?' cried Dr Grace. 'You may well ask!' replied the collier. 'It was that big son of yours!' Dr Grace

---

* Quoted by the Australian journalist Dave Scott of *The Almanac*. At twenty-one Billy Pocock visited New Zealand with his step-father. Having stayed on, Billy subsequently settled in Australia.

drew the tooth, calmed him down him and sent him home. He was clearly furious, so we hid ourselves.

Dr Henry's desire to discipline Gilbert and Fred was undercut by the vital role marked out for them in the fulfilment of his main ambition: to create and run a Gloucestershire County Cricket Club. One of his biggest challenges was the lack of a suitable ground. As far back as 1863 he had written to the local press suggesting the development of a venue on the common land of Durdham Down (where Clifton Cricket Club alone had permission to play): 'I would suggest that a space five or six times as large as that enclosed by Clifton Club be levelled, re-turfed and enclosed for the use of all cricket clubs, schools and cricketers of Bristol: that the ground be put under the care of a professional cricketer . . .' Nothing, however, had come of it. The Down remained a wilderness and lesser men might have given up, but not Doctor Henry. He turned his West Gloucestershire side into an occasional touring eleven (which also went under the name of the Gentlemen of Gloucestershire), carefully directing his attention towards those who might give financial support to a Grace-centred county club.

Unfortunately not all these goodwill matches ended up achieving their objective, for, as at Knole Park, Dr Henry was constantly struggling to rein in his sons' wildly competitive instincts. There is a Georgian manor house in private residence at Holt, three miles outside Bradford-on-Avon, for example, where in 1867, thanks to the generous hospitality of its owner, Thomas Burton Watkin Forster, the Grace touring eleven arrived for a two-day fixture with Twenty-two of Wiltshire. Carnage ensued. Thomas Forster's lovely cricket ground had never seen anything quite like it as W.G. smote a mighty 95 and E.M. a manic 200. There was no respite. The two elated brothers bowled unchanged, whooping with delight as the Twenty-two of Wiltshire came and went, all out 56. When Wiltshire followed on, there was Fred, furious not to have been given a bowl in the first innings, charging in like the Light Brigade. Poor Watkin Forster, past his prime and used to being given a generous full-toss or two early on, again had his stumps quickly spread-eagled. There were plenty of cries of pain as Fred, thirsting for blood, struck again and again. Holt Manor continued to host country house cricket for several years and, indeed, the ground still exists, but Thomas Forster quietly dissociated himself from any involvement in Dr Henry's ambitious plans.

Boosted by W.G.'s spreading fame, however, Dr Henry persevered and soon marked the new decade with the formation of a Gloucestershire County Cricket Club with himself as Treasurer, E.M. as Secretary, W.G. as Captain, and his son Henry on the Committee. Most importantly, he had persuaded the Duke of Beaufort to accept the Presidency, and in early June 1870 he had the satisfaction of a first-class match against Surrey, a one-off using the Clifton Club's pitch on Durdham Down.

* * *

Today Durdham Down survives as a half-mile strip of public common land, stretching from the River Avon to Stoke Bishop and Redland. We must imagine it even wider, much wilder and more windswept, unencumbered by the surrounding housing. We have come to the eastern end, on Saville Road, and are looking across the well-mown grass from the junction with Hollybush Lane. If we walk out through the trees and across the grass for eighty steps or so, we will be standing on a bumpy football pitch near the wicket on which Dr Henry's Gloucestershire played a strong Surrey team. It was here, too, a week earlier, that Dr Henry had organised a dry run with a minor county, Glamorgan.

* * *

The Surrey match began on a Thursday afternoon. Marches and polkas from a military band helped entice a good crowd to form a noisy ring around a playing-area roughly marked out by flags. There were no fences or screens, so the cricket was free for all, subsidised by the subscriptions Dr Henry had raised. Carriages and traps mingled with marquees, tents and colourful bunting. Word had spread about the strength of the visitors. Surrey's all-professional eleven were captained by Heathfield Harman Stephenson, an experienced thirty-seven-year-old fast bowler, batsman and occasional wicket-keeper who ten years earlier had led the first touring party to Australia. When representing All-England he had once taken three wickets in three balls and been presented with a hat, the feat ever since being called a 'hat-trick'. His Surrey team included the belligerent left-handed all-rounder George Griffith (one of Victorian cricket's several suicides), the experienced batsman Dick Humphrey, and two outstanding talents, both in their late twenties, Harry Jupp (whose dogged determination would result in over 15,000 first-class runs) and the tough little wicket-keeper-batsman Ted Pooley, among whose many off-field crises were scrapes with betting syndicates.

W.G.'s intimidating presence and black beard naturally caught everyone's eye, his physical pre-eminence only matched by his good friend Arthur Bush, an equally huge young man, one of Clifton College's earliest sporting stars. Teddy at twenty-nine was the oldest member of the team, Fred, at nineteen, the youngest, together with Charles Filgate who had just left Cheltenham College. The average age was only twenty-two. For all its youthful promise, Dr Henry's Gloucestershire, fielding no professionals, largely depended on his three sons. Most helpfully in this context, young Fred had made wonderful progress. In 1869, when W.G. had scored nine centuries, Fred (as G.F. Grace) had also made five. All the current talk, of course, was of W.G.'s 197 on Durdham Down the previous week against Glamorgan, which revived memories of last season's 220, when he was playing for Clifton. Meanwhile the most knowledgeable pundits held forth on the 180 he had made for the Gentlemen of the South at The Oval.

W.G. won the toss, and at 1.15 p.m. he and E.M. emerged from the players' tent side by side, W.G. towering over his elder brother, each determined to eclipse the other and be the chief player toasted in champagne that evening. They were facing fast bowler Jim Street at one end and the canny forty-two-year-old spinner, Jimmy Southerton, at the other. Short and stocky with a balding head and straggling side-whiskers, Southerton was a former hairdresser who had become the popular licensee of *The Cricketers* on Mitcham Green. He spun his off-breaks prodigiously with what many people thought was a bent arm.

There was a disastrous start, E.M. rashly holing out second ball. The loudest of all the groans surely emanated from Uncle Alfred. Would Teddy never learn? But W.G. cut Street 'to the tents' for a hard-run 4 and was just beginning to open up when he too was out, caught behind by Pooley off Southerton for 26. Pooley leapt in glee. W.G. glowered in menace. But Surrey had brought their own umpire and W.G. had to go. Two Gloucestershire committee members also fell before the lunch break: Tom Matthews, a debonair twenty-year-old whose father ran a chemical business, and Frank Townsend, who would shortly open his own school in Bristol. Worse followed after lunch. Gloucestershire were bowled out by Southerton and Street for 106. The most cheerful people on the ground were the bookmakers.

As W.G. led Gloucestershire out onto Durdham Down, it was clear that he meant business. Agamemnon before the gates of Troy could not have looked so fierce, though similarly bearded. Opening the bowling with his round-arm, medium-paced in-dippers, W.G. was soon letting the batsmen know that their presence on the field was thoroughly detestable. Fred let fly from the other end with the all-or-nothing thunderbolts that had so distressed Thomas Burton Watkin Forster. Such was their combined ferocity that Harry Jupp, always as cautious during the hours of play as he was incautious after them, remained firmly on 0, and when, after eleven four-ball overs, his partner Dick Humphrey was out, the score was just 1-1. The loquacious Ted Pooley, however, completely unmoved by the Graces' assault, verbal and physical, began spiritedly counter-attacking and when he somehow managed to loft one of W.G.'s better deliveries to the top of the ladies' tent for 4, the explosion could have been heard down in the dockyards. W.G.'s irritation mounted as Pooley's theatricalities continued. There was a further explosion when a Pooley snick ended up in a crowd of spectators who were well inside the field of play and seemed not at all bothered by the protestations of those vainly looking for the ball. A panting Pooley – for he and Jupp had scampered a fair number of runs during this diversion – then imperiously held up play and demanded the removal of the spectators. 'They are blocking me favourite shot, Mr Grace. It really ain't fair!' Both W.G. and Fred by this time were speechless with belligerence. If there had been a pair of forceps to hand, the outcome might have been dire. But the intruders were urged back behind the flags; the game continued; Pooley played his 'favourite shot'; and Filgate, down at long-leg, took a memorable catch. More words were exchanged between the younger Graces and the retreating Surrey wicket-keeper, and so fierce was the reception for all the subsequent batsmen that afternoon that when 6.30 came and stumps were drawn, Surrey had slumped to 82-8.

The second day's play began at noon. A miraculous last-wicket stand featuring Jimmy Southerton, whose defence was non-existent, somehow gave Surrey an important lead. Catch after catch eluded the poor fielders. By the time the damaging stand was at last over, W.G. was in the foulest of tempers. He was even crosser shortly afterwards. The wretched Pooley had claimed to have caught him and, despite his very clear statement that the ball, in touching his pad, had got absolutely nowhere near his bat, that mountebank of a Surrey umpire had had the nerve to disagree. Fortunately Dr Henry's selection of well-coached young players paid off, for, despite few runs from all three Graces, Cheltenham College's Charles Filgate, benefiting from all the advice he had enjoyed from Jem Lillywhite,* enabled the county to set Surrey 140 to win. By the close 110 were needed with 9 wickets left.

A huge crowd gathered on Durdham Down on the Saturday morning when play resumed at 12.20 p.m. with the betting favouring a Surrey win. Harry Jupp was taking no chances on the bone-dry, dusty wicket, happy to spend the entire day, if necessary, in painstaking run-accumulation. W.G. and G.F. huffed and puffed, and if looks could produce wickets, Jupp would have not lasted long. Though one of his partners was removed by E.M.'s brilliant sprint and swallow dive from point – arms outstretched, grasping in his finger-tips a ball from W.G. that had been knocked up on the leg-side without any seeming danger – Jupp pressed on steadily. W.G. began to tire. At this critical moment came vindication of Dr Henry's decision to give the captaincy to W.G. rather than E.M., who had certainly been expecting it. Although as a general rule W.G. tended to over-bowl himself, he was less pig-headed than his brother and now had the good sense to give way to a slow left-armer, Robert Fenton Miles, an Oxford Blue from Marlborough College, in a timely act of self-negation of which E.M. would have been incapable. Shortly afterwards Southerton and Street were both bowled, heaving at Miles, and when Miles and G.F. took the last two wickets, Jupp was left stranded on 50. It was only 2.30 in the afternoon. Surrey had ended 51 runs short. W.G. and Fred had taken 16 wickets between them in the match. The refreshment tents stayed open for a long celebration, and the band played on.

* * *

Station Road, Nottingham, runs parallel with the railway line. As we approach it today from Carrington Road and the Edwardian station buildings, the street is dominated by Jury's Hotel. Not far away from Jury's, in a building long since demolished, was the Summers Commercial Hotel, a small establishment run by the parents of a young Nottinghamshire professional, George Summers. It was ideally placed for business, facing what, in Victorian times, was a large, neoclassical entrance to the station, and it was only a mile away from Trent Bridge.

---

*   James Lillywhite senior, the cousin of the slow bowler Jim (James Lillywhite junior) who played for Sussex and the United South.

Summers, 'a well-spoken, good-looking man with a heavy moustache' seemed more of a gentleman than many of the amateurs, and was always neatly dressed. His mother would send him off to away matches with several bottles of Summers Botanic Beer – a form of ginger beer with added herbs – that she brewed herself and successfully marketed for its prophylactic qualities. Station Road was as proud of the Summers Botanic Beer as it was of young George Summers.

One mile away to the north lies the Nottingham General Cemetery. There in the silence of a summer afternoon in 1870 we can see the tall figure of W.G. dominating a large group of mourners by a graveside where a memorial stone later stated:

> This tablet was erected to the memory of George Summers by the Mary-le-bone Club to mark their sense of his qualities as a cricketer and to testify their regret at the untimely accident on Lord's ground which cut short a career so full of promise, June 19th, 1870, in the 26th year of his age.

* * *

Less than two weeks after Gloucestershire's triumph over Surrey on Durdham Down, Summers had been injured on the third day of Nottinghamshire's match with M.C.C., in whose first innings W.G. had made an undefeated century. Though improvements were being planned, Lord's had notoriously bumpy pitches in 1870. W.G. himself knew it all too well. Just the previous month, in scoring 66 for M.C.C. & Ground, he had braved a terrible assault from the Yorkshire fast bowlers Freeman and Emmett. 'It was a marvel the Doctor was not maimed or unnerved for the rest of his days or killed outright', commented George Freeman later, 'by our expresses flying about his ribs, shoulders and head'. Tom Emmett agreed:

> Freeman and I were at our best and Lord's was at its worst. I verily believe there wasn't one square inch of the Dr. from his ankles up to his shoulders that wasn't black and blue after that score. We barked his shins, battered his thighs, skinned his fingers, rattled his ribs, pounded his chest, thumped his elbow and made a mark on his back; he didn't seem to mind. We have never ceased to wonder that one of us didn't either cut him over or kill him that day.

The story goes that one ball, from which W.G. ducked away, climbed so high it was caught without bouncing by the long-stop.

Summers had done well in the first innings, featuring in a second-wicket stand of over 100 with his captain Richard Daft and doggedly defending maiden after maiden from W.G. In his second innings, however, the first ball he received from M.C.C.'s fast bowler John Platts rose up fiercely, possibly after hitting a small stone, and struck him on one side of his head, just over the ear, knocking him unconscious. Everyone rushed up and W.G. pronounced that he still had a pulse. Having been carried off the field, he recovered consciousness, spent the night in his hotel and then took the train home, where, three days later, he collapsed and died.

The tragedy of George Summers did much to encourage a general improvement in the quality of pitches throughout the country which was reflected in steadily higher scores. It is a reminder, too, of just how remarkable W.G.'s run-making was in the 1870s.

* * *

1870 had proved another brilliant year for W.G. who topped the country's averages again with an astonishing 54.78. 'The magnificent batting of Mr W.G. Grace,' declared *Lillywhite's Companion*, was 'the leading feature of the season ... Being possessed of great reach, and never puzzled by the best bowling, his placing of the ball is perhaps the most remarkable feature of his batting, marvellous as is his defence and well-timed his hitting.' He was the 'quickest run-getter and surest batsman in England'.

* * *

It is time to visit the W.G. Grace on Bristol's Whiteladies Road, a pub that was opened in 2012 after a £1.1 million refit by J.D. Wetherspoon. It may be a disappointment that there is no picture of a man with a beard on the pub sign, and that inside visual tributes are limited to two framed photos on the shelves of 'The W.G. Grace book and games club', but W.G. would surely approve of the thriving and friendly atmosphere. It is also admirably sited, close to Clifton College, whose cricket ground Dr Henry had had his eyes on for some time. At last, in August 1871, nine years after the school was opened, the county of the Graces played their first match there, entertaining Nottinghamshire.

Dr Henry's star batsman was in his usual outstanding form in 1871. The Arctic weather of the early months had not prevented 181 at Lord's for M.C.C., 118 for the Gentlemen of the South at West Brompton, 178 for The South at Lord's and 162 for the Gentlemen of England at Fenner's. He had done well too in Gloucestershire's first two matches of the season – a week spent in London, playing M.C.C. and Surrey. He had top-scored in both innings in the 5-wicket victory at Lord's and although he had not come off at The Oval, he and E.M. had bowled the county to a famous innings victory. The week had been notable, too, for a fourth Grace in the Gloucestershire ranks, eldest brother Henry. More recently, W.G. had amassed 189 not out for The Single versus The Married at Lord's as well as a new record score for The Oval, 268 for South versus North.

Dr Henry, therefore, was feeling extremely confident as he and the family journeyed to Clifton College for that important first fixture in August 1871.

He was excited, too, by the attractive solution to his problems: the use in the summer holidays of the Close, the Clifton College ground (that was soon to be immortalised by Henry Newbolt's poem with the famous lines, 'Play up! play up! and play the game!'). It had so much more to offer than Durdham Down: gate receipts via the use of enclosure; a splendid architectural backdrop of Chapel and Big School; a high-class social ambience; and a new relationship with a ready source of good young amateurs.

* * *

With the sun shining and the toss won, W.G. and E.M. strode out at 12.35 to provide a glorious morning's entertainment. When the lunch bell rang at 2.15, the brothers had put on 129, with W.G. on 78, outpacing E.M. on 51, after a hard-fought battle with the two unrelated Shaws: thirty-five-year-old Jem, a fast left-hander with a higher arm than most of his contemporaries, and twenty-eight-year-old Alfred, one of the great leaders and entrepreneurs among Victorian professionals, whose right-arm slow-medium had a nagging length and subtle variations of pace. This talented Notts pair, who together bowled 250 four-ball overs in the match, were always treated with respect by W.G., though Jem was to say in exasperation on one famous occasion, 'I puts the ball where I likes and he puts it where he likes.'

That morning, it was W.G.'s belligerence, rather than E.M.'s, that caught the eye: cutting Alfred Shaw down 'over the ridge' for 3, and then again to the Big School wall; driving Jem Shaw so hard the ball flew past the stumbling Oscroft and beyond the palings, down College Road for 4; powering Jem past point for an all-run 4; repeating this off successive balls, each shot soaring 'clean over the boundary for 4'; crashing three imperious on-drives to the pavilion off fast bowler William Elliott; and running nimbly down the wicket to Richard Daft, to meet the Notts skipper's lobs, placing them unerringly between fielders. Throughout the innings, anything pitched short he pulled round dismissively to square-leg.

The county's first-ever lunch at the College ground was a wonderful social occasion with the family to the fore. Hordes of friends and admirers toasted the champion. W.G. responded with equal enthusiasm. Watching from a distance, Dr Henry knew that he had another worry to share with Martha. Gilbert was drinking far too heavily for his own good. It was bad enough in the evenings when play was over, but at lunchtime it was positively idiotic. He was surrounded by similarly self-indulgent friends, like big Arthur Bush. When the season was over, he must have a good heart-to-heart with Gilbert to sort it all out. In the meantime he must do something about shortening the lunchbreaks. This first one had gone on for eighty minutes. It was an embarrassment. Notts were out on the field, sitting down and looking ostentatiously bored. And even now W.G. wasn't ready...

Rain meant the game ended in a draw, but there was much to encourage Dr Henry: Gilbert made a responsible 55 in the second innings, one of his several glorious straight drives rushing well past the pavilion. Fred had impressed with a rapid 46 and all three of his sons had bowled very tidily. Townsend, Bush, Matthews and Miles looked well at home in the first-class game, and there were several other promising public school recruits like Filgate, Strachan, Wyatt and Goodwyn – young men preparing for careers in the law, stock exchange, army and church who could also be useful assets.

Two weeks later all the family were back at Clifton for the Surrey match. W.G. had been in the runs again – 117 for M.C.C. and 217 for The Gentlemen – but this time he succumbed to Jimmy Southerton for 23. The county, however, were positioned for their eventual innings victory by a hard-hitting stand between Tom Matthews (201) and Fred (89). The match culminated in Gloucestershire's need to take the final Surrey wickets shortly before the close of play. Because Arthur Bush had been injured, W.G. had been keeping wicket in alternate bursts with E.M. And just as he had ended the Surrey first innings with two stumpings, so, too, he had the satisfaction of winning the game with a catch and another stumping.

Dr Henry and Martha, looked back on the season with mixed feelings. Gilbert and Fred were continuing to add to their national reputations. With the possibility of long-term summer use of the Close at Clifton, the county's future looked very promising, too. If only Gilbert and Fred would live more sensibly, they could have been content. But the season had ended with rumours of wild betting at the return fixture with Notts at Trent Bridge. The bookmakers there had been offering long odds against W.G. scoring a century and all three sons had snapped up as many offers as they could get. It was another topic that Dr Henry would have to raise over the winter. For the time being, he and Martha could console themselves with the publication of the national averages. Gilbert, in addition to taking 79 wickets, had scored 2,739 runs, including ten centuries, at an unprecedented average of 78. And second, with an average of 44, came twenty-year-old Fred. *Lillywhite's Companion* this time wrote of 'the Champion Cricketer' whose 'equal has never been seen'.

* * *

Unfortunately, the heart-to-heart talks between anxious father and errant son did not, in the end, take place. The one-sided battle of wills was over. Dr Henry had worn himself out, and two days before Christmas 1871 he succumbed to pneumonia at The Chesnuts. The short illness was precipitated by his characteristic determination to do the right thing at all times, both socially and professionally. He had insisted on riding out to hounds despite a heavy cold, after which he had stayed up all night with an ailing patient.

He was buried across the road at Christ Church, where a white marble tablet was later put up on the bare walls with a formal tribute:

In
Sacred and loving
Remembrance of
Henry Mills Grace,
Surgeon in the Parish for 40 years,
Highly respected and deeply regretted
By all classes throughout the
County of Gloucester.
Died 23rd December 1871, Aged 63

The *Clifton Chronicle* noted that 'few better sportsmen existed' and he would be much missed by the members of the Beaufort and Berkeley Hunts. 'He was beloved for his professional kindness towards the poor, no less than for the generosity of his disposition and the genial way in which he demeaned himself towards everyone with whom he came into contact'. All in all, the son of Ashton Court's unreliable butler had come a long way.

5

A Tour and a Wedding

From North America to West Brompton, 1872–73

In August 1872 W.G. embarked at Liverpool on his first overseas tour, a two-month expedition to Canada and the United States, led by M.C.C.'s secretary Robert Fitzgerald. We have come to the M.C.C. Library at Lord's to learn more about it. Fitzgerald's private scrapbook of the tour was presented to the club by his grandson in the early 1950s. It bulges with all the newspaper reports and related letters and mementoes crammed in within its time-worn red leather covers.

* * *

Fitzgerald was an ideal front-man in the turbulent Canada of the 1870s, for he was fluent in French and German, yet, at the same time, had aristocratic connections and a Harrow and Cambridge background that would have delighted the most reactionary of the colonial English. He had always nursed ambitions as a writer, dramatist and lyricist, and on his return he pored over his scrapbook to write a lively account of the tour, *Wickets In The West*. He later pasted into the scrapbook his publisher's bill with a comment on the loss he had made of £101 6s 11d. 'Paid with a heavy sigh, but proud to add my name to the long list of Calamitous Authors'. The scrapbook and *Wickets*, far from being calamitous, together provide a fascinating insight into a controversial tour that W.G. would always maintain was one of the happiest experiences of his life.

The idea of visiting North America was not new. George Parr had taken over an all-professional Twelve in 1859, and another one, led by Edgar Willsher in 1868, played Canada at Montreal in addition to several matches (of baseball as well as cricket) in the USA. On both occasions the local twenty-twos had been overwhelmed by the tourists, and this was probably why a team of twelve amateurs, led by Fitzgerald himself, was requested when Thomas Patteson, a lawyer and Toronto newspaper editor, travelled to Lord's from Canada in the summer of 1871 with an exciting new proposal.

Patteson,* who would manage the tour and invest $1,500 in the speculation, was an Englishman who had emigrated to Canada as a young man. He had made neither the Eton nor Oxford eleven but had captained Canada against the USA. His offer was attractive: $600 in gold for each player for half a dozen matches in Canada; all expenses liberally looked after and also paid in gold; first-class travel throughout; and the likelihood of a few remunerative matches in the USA. If it would be helpful for recruitment purposes, a few days' holiday could be included at the Niagara Falls at the exclusive Clifton House hotel, but the whole project totally depended on the presence of W.G. in the Twelve. Without England's champion cricketer to bring the crowds in, the tour was a non-starter.

On getting Fitzgerald's agreement in principle, Patteson sent a colleague, Captain Nesbit Wallace, down to Bristol on a mission to secure W.G. for the tour. Wallace had wide connections, having played much high-class club cricket in England in the 1860s and went down so well at The Chesnuts that he was included in two of Gloucestershire's fixtures that summer of 1871. Perhaps he undid all his good work, however, by hardly troubling the scorers at either Clifton or Trent Bridge. At all events, W.G. prevaricated, and a letter from Patteson, pasted into Fitz's scrapbook, shows that as late as April 1872 the tour was still in some doubt:

My dear Mr Fitzgerald
I am literally besieged with the enquiry 'Are the English Gentlemen coming out?' and my life is rendered a burden to me. Pray let me know the latest news on the subject . . .

Eventually it was agreed at Downend that G.F. should stay behind with Martha, allowing W.G. to embrace the new adventure.

The 'English Gentlemen' who finally made the nine-day crossing of the Atlantic were a youthful group with only two outstanding cricketers to back up W.G.: the hard-hitting Old Harrovian Albert ('Monkey') Hornby and left-handed Arthur Appleby (nicknamed by Fitz 'The Tormentor'), the finest amateur fast bowler of the time, praised for his smooth action. Both played for the emerging county of Lancashire, where their families happened to run prosperous mills. Three others, however, often represented the Gentlemen against the Players: skilful lob-bowler William Molyneux Rose ('Billy, the blue-blooded buck'); the stylish right-hander and fellow Old Etonian Alfred Lubbock; and 'Frantical Fitz' himself, by far the oldest at thirty-eight. The other half of the party were all undergraduates,

---

*   T.C. Patteson's brief moment in cricket history has tended to become blurred. Not only is his name often misspelt – one biographer delightfully features Mr Pottieson – but also, when Fitzgerald published his account of the tour, he carelessly gave him the initials of his cousin, Bishop J.C. Patteson, an understandable error, for the poor Bishop made headline news that summer by being dramatically martyred in the Solomon Isles. Fitzgerald's error was subsequently repeated by W.G.'s *Reminiscences* and poor T.C. has been given the Bishop's initials of J.C. ever since.

including four more Old Etonians: Edgar Lubbock, a fast underarm bowler and recent member of the winning side of football's inaugural F.A. Cup; Cuthbert Ottaway, who was to participate in three Cup Finals and would shortly be captain in England's first international match; the Hon. George Harris, soon to become the 4th Baron Harris and, later, captain both Kent and England; and Francis Percy Umfreville Pickering, whose uncle had organised the tour of 1859. Old Harrovian Walter Hadow (already celebrated for a double century with Middlesex) and Old Rugbeian Charles ('Frolicksome') Francis had both been schoolboy cricket prodigies. Amid the plethora of nicknames, Fitzgerald dubbed W.G. 'the Unapproachable' – fitting recognition of the massive gap in ability between him and the other eleven. In 1872, for the fifth successive season, he had been top of the country's averages.

The scrapbooks contain accounts of matches against twenty-twos at Montreal, Ottawa, Toronto, London and Hamilton as well as across the border, in New York, Philadelphia and Boston. The first fixture set the tone. After the Twelve had amassed 255 (W.G. top-scoring with 81), the Montreal twenty-two were bowled out for 48 and 67, Billy Rose taking 33 wickets with his lobs, eight of which were stumpings by Cuthbert Ottaway. Over the ten matches W.G. showed star quality on very indifferent pitches, averaging just under 50 and even making one score of 142. The next highest average was 16. He also took large clutches of wickets as the first-change bowler (13-35, for example, in Boston's second innings), though the wiles of Rose and the speed of Appleby often left him with little to do. It was light-hearted and largely one-sided cricket against weak opposition. 'Many wickets fell to longhops,' admitted Fitzgerald, 'such as would never have bowled a boy at a small school in England.'

The devotion with which Fitz pasted into his scrapbook a wide variety of non-cricketing memorabilia – from drinking songs and dance invitations to menus and wine lists – shows the importance he attached to the rich off-field entertainment. Toronto, where there was 'cricket by day, dinners and dancing by night', was typical. *Wickets*, too, chronicles an awesome abundance of food and drink. The welcoming banquet at Montreal was 'sumptuous'; the first meal in New York 'a dinner fit for gods'. Problems could always be ameliorated by 'a few bottles of champagne', successes enhanced by 'a copious supply'. Steam could be let off by 'a wild career for a few hours'. Canadian cocktails were widely enjoyed and the good news was 'they do you just as much good at daybreak as at any hour', while the bars in Montreal provided the delightful revelation that 'there was no thimbleful or imperial pint' for 'the bottle is given to you and you help yourself'. There was quality as well as quantity, many of the hotels providing a breadth of vintage wines that W.G. would have rarely, if ever, have seen. Dining at the Niagara Falls, he was able to indulge his thirst for champagne from a choice that included Mumm's Dr Verzenay, Roederer's Carte Blanche, Moet and Chandon, Heidsieck and Piper. The fine clarets – St Julien, Margaux, Leoville, Latour and Lafite – would likewise have been irresistible. There was much more besides.

Fitz's good-time agenda of wine, women and song was facilitated by letters from friends in England to influential Canadians. One such missive declared:

He is accompanied by the nicest lot of young Englishmen Quebec has seen for many a day and if the Fair Ladies of Quebec are not all away at the seaside you must give them an opportunity of capturing or being captured in the good old city which has always been famous for that sort of thing . . .

Wickets is awash with indications of the team's roving eyes. On the voyage out, travelling first-class, they enjoyed 'walks of discovery', searching for pretty girls among passengers in the steerage. When Appleby was seen 'in familiar conversation with a young lady whose unprotected state led to offers of consolation', others swiftly muscled in. The coffee-room of one hotel was full of 'all that was beautiful in Ottawa'. When shooting the rapids there on rafts, 'the Twelve placed themselves at the mercy of several Circes', 'clinging to a waist not loth to be pressed'. The same Ottawa lovelies later enjoyed an 'impromptu hop in the coffee-room that was kept up with spirit till 4 a.m.'.

At Brockville Fitz and Appleby enjoyed a post-dinner tryst, walking a couple of unchaperoned fair ones home. There was a similar lack of chaperones in Toronto when a party of ninety took part in a day's excursion to Lake Simcoe. At one lakeside stop their boat steamed off, leaving behind a 'distinguished member of the Twelve and his young lady', who had gone off by themselves 'unconscious of everything'. W.G., the most distinguished member of the Twelve, was later seen surrounded by a bevy of admiring Toronto ladies as he waited to go into bat and, when a wicket fell, was so moved by their entreaties to stay and chat that the unthinkable occurred and he ceded his turn at the wicket to someone else. When he eventually did go in, he smashed 27 from seven balls and the cries of disappointment from his new fans were almost as loud as his own vehement protestations when the pyrotechnics were halted by an unfortunate lbw decision. At London, however, where he and Fitz were challenged to croquet by 'two fair ladies', he displayed a little less chivalry. When the girls let slip that they were the current district champions, W.G.'s implacable will to win made the exchange of sweet nothings an impossibility. Nonetheless, there were tearful scenes when they left Toronto: 'the pressure of one, if not more than one, warm hand said all that words could say or the heart could feel.' It was at Toronto that three of the Twelve opted to stay an extra day – 'the amorous Appleby', Ottaway and Francis – consequently missing the start of the next game. Only a few years later, Ottaway was married in Canada to a Miss Stinson, whom he had met on the tour at Hamilton. When Fitz's poetic Alphabet in the scrapbook comes to O and P, however, it reveals his wicket-keeper fighting for the affections of another fair lady:

Ottoway smit with the charm of Miss Fraser;[*]
Pickering equally ready to praise her.

Fitz took a great interest in ensuring an adequate number of fair ladies along the way:

I am the idiot who took the lads over.
J is the Joy when I land 'em in clover.

The scrapbook, however, reminds us of the inhibiting formality of the times, and that the 'clover', on many occasions, was probably of limited bliss. At a ball at the Royal Hotel, Hamilton, for example, each participant was given an attractive printed 'card' containing the evening's twenty dances – a mixture of quadrilles, lancers, waltzes and galops, often featuring Offenbach and Strauss' latest hits. (They regularly waltzed to 'The Blue Danube'.) The card contained spaces in which to mark the name of the partner to whom each dance had been promised, though the scrapbook's card is empty of entries. Perhaps Fitz defied convention and danced with the current apple of his eye all night. W.G., at six foot two, was a prominent figure on the ballroom floor and, at only twelve and half stone, a lithe one too. We read that at Government House, Quebec, 'the excellent ballroom was crowded. Mr Grace, who must now be known by sight to more people in England than even Mr Gladstone, was especially noticeable for the skill and agility of his movements'.

Flirtations, then, played a major part in the entertainment of the tour, but they were probably nothing much more. Victorian respectability decreed that sex was for the married. For unmarried gentlemen it meant love-making below stairs or visits to brothels. 'The chambermaids are remarkable,' wrote Fitz nostalgically of one hotel, praising 'their good looks and civility' . . .

Only three years after the tour, Fitz suffered the onset of a slow, mortal illness. Another of his scrapbooks at Lord's contains tragic entries from his 'madhouse', indicating brave attempts at controlling a troubled mind, as well as the doctor's letter of December 1875 urging him to relinquish his secretarial role at Lord's immediately. Underneath he added poignantly:

My first warning. I placed my resignation in the hands of the committee this afternoon. I was too affected to read my own death warrant. The committee behaved towards me with the greatest kindness . . . everything was arranged to help me in my feeble state.

Five years of insanity followed. His death certificate tells of 'softening of the brain' which usually means tertiary syphilis.

[*]   The surname was omitted, but the odds seem heavily in favour of Miss Fraser.

All this being so, Fitz's account of a tour of New York by gaslight, featuring its gin palaces, almost certainly related to a red light district, where he was doing his usual best to ensure his lads landed up 'in clover'. Fitz admits to being irresistibly drawn into them, describing the invitingly clad waitresses as 'nymphs in no garb of a later date than the palmy days of Lais of Corinth' – an allusion to a famous ancient Greek prostitute. Both repelled and fascinated ('you are disgusted in your delight'), he let fascination win the day, and after the first establishment they tried several others.

On their return the team came under considerable criticism. 'The love of the game' had been blurred, some suggested, by 'an inordinate desire to banquet and carouse at the expense of the poor dependency'. W.G.'s own books tried hard to emphasise the missionary nature of the tour and eliminate any baser suggestions. For well over a hundred years his biographers have dutifully followed his line, but it is hard to take it seriously. The restraining influence of Dr Henry had gone. The Atlantic separated W.G. from all those Christ Church sermons. He could indulge his wild side, completely off the family leash and able to combine some highly remunerative cricket with having a fling and sowing some wild oats. As Fitz led the lascivious dance around North America, like a stout little satyr or mischievous, bearded Pan, W.G. was there among the young initiates, delightedly participating in that glorious Bacchanalia. The whole team, he wrote in *Reminiscences*, agreed that the tour had been wonderfully harmonious. 'I attribute the credit for this very largely to the man we had as our captain . . . and looking back to the tour, over a vista of nearly thirty years, it stands out in the memory as a prolonged and happy picnic.'

A hedonistic spirit of *carpe diem* was understandable in the nineteenth century, when, as W.G., the doctor's son, knew full well, death lay eagerly in wait for the young as well as the old. Not only were the shadows already lengthening around 'Frantical Fitz' but two of his Oxford undergraduates – Ottaway and Pickering, who had enthusiastically vied for the affections of fair Miss Fraser – would not reach thirty.

* * *

With the tourists expected back any day, preparations for W.G.'s return to The Chesnuts were in full swing. Martha's delight was mixed with concern, something she shared each Sunday when the Graces met up at Christ Church. We can see her there at the end of a service, a commanding figure still in mourning black, pausing in the thin September sunshine by her husband's grave as the congregation disperses and she waits for the family: Uncle Alfred right beside her, his beard now totally grey, a regular visitor to his sister's home since Dr Henry's death; John Dann with his walrus moustache and the vivacious Blanche; serious-minded Annie with her doctor husband, who'd just been collecting up the hymn books; twenty-two-year-old Fred, across the churchyard, chatting up a cluster of love-struck admirers and their uneasy chaperones, amused at the tremors aroused in local hearts; his sister Fanny (fated, alas, to arouse few tremors in any heart), moving across to mother, fully cognisant of her latest concerns, having dutifully listened to them many times in the past week. The conversation that ensued is easily imagined.

First, the vexed question of money. There had been disappointment when the Melbourne Cricket Club declared themselves unable to meet Gilbert's terms for bringing a team to Australia, so, financially at least, the North American tour had been a God-send. But Gilbert had been right not to undersell himself. There had not been an Australian tour since George Parr's visit ten years earlier. New offers from Melbourne would probably come Gilbert's way. In the meantime he seemed to be making ends meet, but what would happen – the second question – if and when the resumption of his medical studies occurred? Gilbert's resolute antipathy towards this was an ever increasing worry. Even Teddy, who hardly ever stinted himself on his cricket, had gained all his qualifications by Gilbert's present age.

There was the further question of all the adulation he was getting, the mixing with people above his station and, with it all, the betting and heavy drinking. Was his life becoming too louche? Was there now a real danger of his losing his way both as a person and sportsman? Mr Fitzgerald's patronage, in that respect, was a real anxiety. No-one could be unaware of the whispers circulating in M.C.C. circles about their controversial secretary. Gilbert, at rising twenty-five, needed to get his head out of the clouds and sober up.

This, then, was the cue for John Dann to pronounce with all the solemnity he usually reserved for his introduction of Martha's harp accompaniment to the *Nunc Dimittis* that it might be time for Gilbert to marry. Uncle Alfred, never slow to voice an opinion, swiftly backed him up. What Gilbert needed was not a pretty, empty-headed confection of curls and lace, but someone down-to-earth, level-headed, capable, if necessary, of laying down the law! A Penelope rather than a Calypso. Fred had sauntered over by this stage, and it was surely Fred, who knew Gilbert so well, who now brought up the name of Agnes Nicholls Day.

Agnes, he reminded them, was a relation on the Pocock side of the family and not yet twenty. If the look in Gilbert's eye down at Prince's ground last summer was anything to go by, the dark and attractively sharp-featured Agnes Day might well be in with a chance. She and Gilbert had got to know each other through visits the Days had made to West Brompton's Lillie Bridge ground, where she had watched W.G. on both track and cricket field along with her elder brother James, a talented sportsman. It was probably the thought of foxy-faced Agnes that had made W.G. so keen to play there last year for the Gentlemen of the South and it was to the ladies' marquee that he was spotted doffing his cap on reaching his century. More telling, perhaps, Gilbert had on one or two occasions engineered opportunities for her brother James to play in important first-class matches. He represented the Gents of the South, for example, up at Beeston two years ago against the Gents of the North. Fred remembered it well. He himself had scored

189 not out. Agnes might not have gone up to Nottinghamshire for the match – it was difficult to remember – but overall, everything considered, it had to be a real possibility that the girl had made quite an impression on Gilbert.

* * *

Martha's face lit up. Agnes was the granddaughter of her own eldest sister, the dear late Bessie. Agnes' mother Elizabeth had taught at Bessie's Downend school for a while before marrying and settling down with her husband William Day in Islington. The strong Pocock connection was a big recommendation, but there was a downside: the hard times Agnes' family had been having after William Day had run through a considerable fortune, the rumoured £30,000 that his father, creator of one of the leading lithographic businesses in London, had left him.

Uncle Alfred knew all about this, for he had learnt the lithography business from the Days and had been so close to the family he had been a witness at Agnes' parents' wedding. Martha was right. For some years the firm had continued to produce many books with exquisite illustrations and bindings. 'Day & Son' were synonymous with expensively produced, high quality products. 'They were well-established and reputable,' sighed Uncle Alfred, who had suffered his own misfortunes in business. 'The firm was considered as safe as the Bank of England'. But it wasn't. Agnes' wayward father lacked any business sense at all. In 1866, when she was thirteen, William Day had suffered the humiliation of liquidation. The company's whole stock and assets had been put up for sale in a series of distressing auctions, which were only just coming to an end.

Martha nodded thoughtfully. That particular family crisis was coming back to her. Agnes' family had only been saved from absolute ruin by a kind aunt and uncle, John and Caroline Nicholls. William Day's elder sister, Caroline, had married really well. Her husband had inherited a fortune and invested it shrewdly. Having no family of their own, they were happy to help the Days cope with their fourteen children. They had found them a house in Coleherne Terrace, in one of the fine new estates being built in West Brompton, where they could make a completely fresh start, taking in some boarders, to help make ends meet. So, thanks to Aunt Caroline, there must be hope that Agnes' father might pull himself together again.

Uncle Alfred had a further update. William Day was currently acting as a part-time agent for his brother John, who also had his own publishing company and had just set up a new business near The Strand. It sounded quite promising. So many businesses seemed to come and go these days. A phoenix usually arose from the ashes when the Pocock family was involved.

Fred had the last word. His mother was quite right about Aunt Caroline. She absolutely doted on her niece. No doubt about it. And from what he'd heard from his chum James Day, the Nicholls weren't just rich. They were stinking rich.

The discussion in due course broke up. There was much to mull over. But one thing looked clear. If Gilbert really had a soft spot for Agnes, then, all things considered, it was probably to be encouraged. He was, after all, her cousin-once-removed and second uncle. It all seemed quite satisfactory.

* * *

Shortly afterwards at The Chesnuts, W.G., safely back from his travels, was sounded out. Little encouragement was needed and early in 1873 the engagement was announced. He and Agnes would be married in October, just in time to go off together to Australia, for a new Melbourne syndicate had asked him to lead a team there, and, although his terms were just as exceptionally high as before, this time, such was his reputation, they had actually been accepted. Agnes had enjoyed the matches she had seen at Prince's, Lord's and Lillie Bridge. She was soon to see a great deal more.

* * *

By 1873 the United South of England Eleven had become an important part of W.G.'s complex cricketing arrangements. Since that first game at Southgate, Willsher and Lillywhite had been keen to recruit him for more matches. W.G. obliged. More than that, he and G.F made a take-over, running the United South themselves and arranging fixtures in the gaps in their first-class commitments. That year, for example, they visited Thame, Edinburgh, Darlington, Alexandra Park, Manchester, Bradford, Leicester, Wakefield, Coventry, Southsea, Lincoln, Inverness, Aberdeen, Northampton, Dublin and Nunhead. It involved remorseless rail travel, but there were good financial deals to be made.

We have caught up with W.G. at the Racecourse Parade Ground, Northampton, where the United South were taking on a local Eighteen, a game revealing the stress he was under three weeks before the wedding and the challenges awaiting Agnes. The racecourse was a huge, sprawling area of grazing land, available for cricket and football whenever there was no racing. The town's leading club (Northamptonshire) was funding the United South's visit. The two Graces cost big money but the Northamptonshire committee hoped to attract crowds of over 5,000, for W.G. was again the country's outstanding batsman, 'undoubtedly the most wonderful cricketer that has ever donned flannels'. They just needed good weather. Unfortunately the match days were wet and cold, with the flat, open expanses of the racecourse at their most uninviting.

* * *

The Racecourse Parade Ground had the use of a fine three-storeyed pavilion, next to the horses' parade ring, built in the early nineteenth century to provide a comfortable view for the more privileged punters. It is now Grade II listed and its central floor has been transformed into an oriental Jade Pavilion dispensing

Thai and Chinese food. Its run-down ground floor has been taken over by an environmentally concerned community co-operative, working enthusiastically towards providing a family-friendly vegetarian café and a renovated space for community meetings and events.

Of the ground itself there is no sign, most of it lying under tennis courts. But the old atmosphere has survived in the flat open spaces of today's 'racecourse' – over a hundred acres of public park, a huge, green oasis in the centre of Northampton.

* * *

The first day proved distinctly inauspicious. The United South, put in to bat on a wet wicket, made an indifferent, rain-interrupted start, though W.G. struggled through to lunch. Pouring rain seriously prolonged the interval and, when it eased, W.G. headed off to the racecourse fairground, run by local gypsies, soon finding plenty of stalls to satisfy his competitive instincts. Time passed, the skies cleared to blue, and W.G. was wielding a productive rifle at a shooting gallery, when a spectator, a local builder, suggested, perhaps a little tartly, that he should keep the crowd waiting no longer but go out and play some cricket. W.G., who had no great liking for batting on mud, was deeply offended. Rude words were exchanged. Words led to blows and, by the time they had been parted, W.G. had sustained a cut face. 'Who's done that, Gilbert?' cried Fred, as his brother returned to the pavilion with blood on his cheek. 'Oh, that cad over there by the entrance,' muttered W.G. grimly. 'Well if you don't go and give him a good hiding,' responded G.F. '*I* certainly shall!' At this, W.G. strode back to the entrance and summarily 'punished the builder with sledge-hammer blows' so that 'the claret in his eyes darkened and closed up in no time'. It provided wonderful entertainment for the cricket-starved spectators who gave W.G. generous applause. There were more cheers, too, at 4.30, when he resumed his innings. The local press reported on the excellent 45 he made out of the Eleven's 102, but kept tactfully quiet about the attack on the builder.

The last two days, cold again and damp, brought in crowds of up to 2,000, but there was little hope of the Northamptonshire committee recuperating their heavy expenses. They were, moreover, sorely tried by an unhelpfully elongated lunch interval on the third day. The *Mercury* later explained the problem. It had been 'necessary that the Articles of Agreement between the players selected by Mr W.G. Grace to proceed next month to Australia to represent our island in the Antipodes should be signed' for 'Mr Grace had arranged that the northern players should meet those of the south in this town for that purpose.' He was accordingly given a special room in the pavilion 'for the players to attend during the luncheon hour and sign the agreement...'

The professionals, who had already let it be known that the financial deal was unattractive, were hardly best pleased by this peremptory summons. The lunch interval ran on and on as W.G. waited, but still there was no sign of Albert

Shaw, Ted Pooley or Tom Emmett. Only Arthur Greenwood and William Oscroft eventually turned up from the railway station, though five others – Martin McIntyre, Harry Jupp, Jimmy Southerton, Dick Humphrey and Jim Lillywhite – were conveniently involved in the Northampton game. Angry at being held to ransom by professionals, W.G. let it be known he would fill the last three places on the tour with amateurs. He quickly signed up his friend Arthur Bush, his young cousin Walter Raleigh Gilbert, and 21-year-old Ferrington Holker Boult of Epsom College and Surrey, who would be obliging enough to stand aside and act as umpire whenever asked. They would all make splendid travelling companions for Fred, Agnes and himself.

One of the contracts signed during the lunch interval at Northampton survives in a private collection (Roger Mann's). Its copperplate hints at the involvement of Uncle Alfred, and there are suggestions of further outside help from the legalistic, no-nonsense approach that 'William Gilbert Grace of Downend, Gentleman' adopted towards his professionals. They were to report to him personally at Southampton on the day before departure. Throughout the tour of 'about 100 days' they were to place themselves 'under the entire disposal and directions of the said William Gilbert Grace and to obey all his orders', playing in 'each of the aforesaid 14 Cricket matches if required by the said William Gilbert Grace so to do'. They would receive £150, paid in three instalments, in addition to a free second-class return P. & O. passage and hotel accommodation as well as travelling and all other expenses, with the sensible exception of 'wines, spirits and other liquors' for which the limit was to be £20. W.G. himself was to do rather better. His fee from the Melbourne Syndicate was £1,500. In addition, he and Agnes would both be reimbursed for their expenses and travel first-class.

As the match at damp Northampton reached its conclusion, the United South looked anything but united. The skipper's mood became darker than the clouds above as wickets tumbled rather quicker than they might have done had the disgruntled professionals been more inclined to sell themselves dearly. When his own unlucky dismissal was compounded by Fred's, out to a brilliant one-handed catch in the deep from a towering hit, the game was up. The Northampton Eighteen had gained a famous victory. Agnes was shortly to gain a handful of a husband.

* * *

They were married on Thursday 9 October 1873 at St Matthias' Church, West Brompton, just round the corner from where the Days lived in Coleherne Road. The attractive terraced houses of Coleherne Road still survive, but St Matthias' was knocked down in the late 1950s.

The loss of the scene of the wedding seems symbolic of Agnes' general exclusion from her husband's story. The vanishing act began in her lifetime, with W.G. exercising a heavy restraint on what Brownlee included in his biography. Brownlee had known Agnes by then for several years and could have put her into proper focus, but, instead, had to be content with a few coy platitudes.

> Happy, happy he who can say I have found one who is in touch with me in work and sorrow, who, in a thousand nameless ways, has made life a charm, and revealed all that is implied in the words 'Home, sweet home'. W.G. is one of the happy fortunate ones, for his wife, with her gentle, womanly touch and sympathy, has made life a beautiful thing to him. She is heart and soul with him in everything he undertakes, and her ways and home are pleasant to the hearts of his friends.

Brownlee begged to be shown the diary that W.G. had kept in the year of his marriage, but W.G. firmly refused, even though 'there was a timid half-consent in the eyes of Mrs Grace that told of such beautiful things to be seen there'. The exclusion was to last a lifetime. Though married to W.G. for forty-two years, Agnes was to receive but three passing references in the whole of the *Memorial Biography*, to which, of course, she was not invited to contribute. In his preface, the chief editor, Sir Home Gordon, gave a telling explanation of the thinking of the day:

> There is nothing in the following pages about the private life of Grace. Alike as son, as brother, as husband and as father, in every relationship of family existence he was exemplary. Those cherished memories are not for the general reader, because the honoured privacy of his domesticity has nothing to do with the public career of the great sportsman.

Subsequent biographers, with so little material to hand, have struggled to present anything but a ghostly paragon of accommodating Victorian womanhood. No doubt it is just possible that the marriage, as Bernard Darwin asserted, was 'a 'perfectly happy union with an affection on both sides that remained fresh and youthful to the end'.* But did Agnes really have the powers of an enchantress who could cast such a spell on the combative national hero that the moment he came through the front door his whole personality changed? It would seem unlikely.

* * *

We have emerged from the Warwick Road exit of Earls Court Station to begin our attempted recreation of the wedding. Across the road is the Earls Court Exhibition Centre, but it is turning in our imagination to open countryside in mellow autumnal colours. We turn left down the Warwick Road, pass Penywern Road and stop at the second turning on the left, Earls Court Square. Across the road is

---

*   Factual errors within the book suggest a certain caution.

a primary school playground protected by high walls from Warwick Road's heavy traffic, but we are back in 1873 and that nondescript playground has become a church of bright, brand-new red brick. We are in the middle of a building site, that part of the West Brompton countryside that is currently in the process of urbanisation in the wake of a flood of development sweeping towards Earls Court and soon to spread far beyond. Before us, horse-drawn wagons loaded with material to aid the completion of Earls Court Square mingle with the carriages of the many Graces, Days and their friends arriving for the wedding. With a certain amount of surmise added to many disparate scraps of information, we, too, will be able to share Gilbert's and Agnes' big day.

W.G. had arrived the night before to stay with friends and family at the Coleherne Arms, conveniently situated at the junction of Coleherne Road and the Old Brompton Road. It still stands, proudly displaying its foundation date of 1866, though now transformed into a 'gastro pub' and renamed the Pembroke, disguising a somewhat bohemian past that included a notorious 'leather bar', Freddie Mercury and Rudolf Nureyev. From there, on the morning of the wedding, W.G. had set out on foot with his Best Man, Arthur Bush. Called 'Frizzy' by his friends because of his luxuriant side-whiskers, the twenty-three-year-old Bush, son of an army officer and born in India, was working in a minor capacity in the family's flourishing warehouse business in Bristol, but, like W.G., able to devote himself primarily to sport. He had already won the first of several rugby football caps for England and was also a fine sprinter, fives player, swimmer and boxer.

A minute later the two men were sighted approaching the church with giant strides and noisy banter. Their teeth glinted in their swarthy pirates' faces. Their top-hats, though dwarfed by their huge frames, still caught the eye for their rakish angles. W.G. was out for a good time. The church's western end faced directly onto Warwick Road, but the piratical pair diverted down a lane at the side of St Matthias', for the vicar, the Revd Samuel Haines, who had funded the building with some adroit financial manoeuvres, had determined on doorways in the side streets to avoid 'the gathering of idle persons around the entrance'. Haines was of passionately high-church conviction, and a pungent aroma of fresh cement, paint and incense met groom and best man as they entered and were ushered in by a smiling James Day to the front of the two wide blocks of oak pews. A recently qualified chemist, James Day had only two weeks earlier been in 'W.G. Grace's Eleven' at Gravesend, playing Kent.

St. Matthias' as yet lacked internal decoration to offset its ubiquitous red brick. It had been designed by an architect whose frugal exercises in Gothic Revival had the advantage, for those with tight budgets, of being able to be built in separate sections. Thus the Revd Haines had built a chancel four years ago and added a timber-roofed nave in 1871. The year after the wedding he would obtain some narrow side-aisles, but the bubble of his precarious finances would finally burst and he never achieved his coveted clock-tower and spire.

The chancel was currently having its ceiling altered and was out of use for the ceremony, forcing the two priests to operate from the front of the nave. John Dann was, in fact, taking the service and the Revd Haines hovering around unhappily on the fringe. When W.G. had learnt that St Matthias' incense-laden services often lasted two hours or more, he had let it be known that the Graces would be producing their own man. (He was always keen to provide his own umpire.) John Dann could be relied upon for pithy sermons. Indeed, on days when there happened to be gym shoes showing underneath his surplice, his impending tennis commitments would make them pithier than ever. As the church began to fill, the Revd Haines eyed the congregation with the baleful look of an opening bowler relegated to third man after just one xxx. He clutched his rosary with fervour as he tried hard to feel sympathetic towards the swelling numbers of deep-tanned, hearty young men exchanging noisy pleasantries with their pretty and brightly-coloured companions. At least their voices drowned out 'Hold The Fort' and other unseemly revivalist hymns being fiercely thumped out on his precious new organ by a plump lady from Bristol who was said to be the groom's eldest sister. His own worst nightmares were being realised. Moody and Sankey had invaded West Brompton.

He had been anxious about the Graces, for it was his belief that most sportsmen tended towards philistinism. He felt sorry, too, for the bride's father, who, though careless of money, had to his credit a catalogue of highly artistic creations. Owen Jones' *The Grammar of Ornament* had already become the classic book of reference on contemporary aesthetics. Then there had been that well-illustrated volume on *The Holy Land*. His brother's publications likewise included the five parts of *Christ is Coming*. The Days were a cultivated family, and there was always a faint chance – one had to be positive – that a little of it might yet brush off on the raffishly-dressed giant of a bridegroom.

19 Coleherne Road, a double-fronted house of four storeys, was a scene of great joy as Agnes and her father waved goodbye from a pony and trap. The cook and housemaid were leading the cheering from the upper windows and the Days' boarders and a host of other well-wishers loyally applauded from around the steps at the front door. William Day had struggled not to feel the house a serious come-down after Grosvenor Lodge, Islington, where they had once had stockbrokers and judges for neighbours, and he would have been surprised to learn that, two centuries on, the four flats that made up his old home would together be worth £4 million. Off they trotted, down the road, turning left at the Coleherne Arms, and right into Warwick Road. In just a minute it was time for the big entrance.

The church was packed. John Dann (no gym shoes visible) started the service. W.G. gave his young bride the kind of encouraging look usually reserved for the arrival of a nervous batting partner. Agnes, however, seemed calm and assured, clearly believing a long partnership a certainty. Sitting near the front, Aunt Caroline and her husband John Nicholls smiled proprietorily, while Martha and Uncle Alfred glowed at the power of the lusty, uninhibited singing. Even the Revd Haines began to look more relaxed – perhaps these cricketers had something to offer, after all? – and hardly flinched when E.M.'s tenor vibrato rose powerfully above everyone, as it always did during his favourite hymn:

Tell me the same old story when you have cause to fear
That this world's empty glory is costing me too dear.
Yes, and when that world's glory is dawning on my soul,
Tell me the old, old story: 'Christ Jesus makes thee whole.'
Tell me the old, old story, tell me the old, old story,
Tell me the old, old story, of Jesus and His love.

In keeping with a young people's service, full of hope and confidence, the register was signed by Agnes' closest sister, eighteen-year-old Marian, and an old Bristol friend of W.G's, John Lloyd, who had been a medical apprentice staying at The Chesnuts at the time of Dr Henry's death and was to rise to the rank of Surgeon-Colonel in the R.A.M.C. Under the heading of 'profession' W.G. had put 'gentleman' rather than 'cricketer'. Agnes gave her address, surprisingly, as 51 Warwick Road. There was only a fortnight between the wedding and departure for Australia, so she may well have been borrowing a friend's home for a London honeymoon. W.G. in his twin capacity as captain and manager would have had much to do in the final days and Earls Court would have made an excellent base.

The service was over. W.G. led his bride down the circuitous route to the side door, while sister Annie fought a fierce fight with that challenging tune by Mendelssohn that Queen Victoria's daughter had so popularised. The most significant event in W.G.'s whole life had just ended.

6

An Extended Honeymoon

With Agnes in Australia, 1873–74

Agnes was a well-informed twenty-year-old, mature for her years. Her hard-working mother, now a boarding-house keeper in all but name, had ensured that she gave herself no false airs or graces. Her head-in-the-clouds father had given her a sense of fun. Her eldest brother William, whose blindness would be no impediment to his vocation as a missionary preacher, had inspired a love of literature and a breadth of interests. Her jaunty brother James had filled her in on every single detail about the great game of cricket. And her devoted Aunt Caroline was always there reassuringly in the background, gently encouraging, a real-life fairy godmother. If anyone could cope with the strangely paradoxical personality of the champion cricketer, wild yet kindly, obstinate but generous, extrovert and vulnerable, it was Agnes.

From Warwick Road she quietly and meticulously prepared for their seven-month absence from England with Gilbert beside her, proudly exultant: in the size of his fee from his Melbourne backers; in the style in which they would now be living; in the wisdom of his mother and the charm of The Chesnuts; and, of course, in his determination to be the best of husbands. A day before embarkation, the couple arrived at the Southampton Docks Station and made for the exclusive Imperial Hotel (later renamed the South Western), built with first-class passengers in mind, and destined to host the farewell parties of those sailing in the *Titanic*.

* * *

The Southampton Docks Station, run in the 1870s by the London and South Western Railway, is now a casino. The Imperial, next door to it, also survives, though it ceased to be a hotel in 1939 and, as South Western House, has recently been converted into luxury apartments. The building has retained its ambience of spacious opulence remarkably well. The old hotel's entrance, staircases and communal rooms still radiate Victorian grandeur with their rich marble columns, wood-panelling and moulded ceilings. Shepherded around the Imperial's lavish lounges, bars and ballroom by a husband resolutely ensuring that their last hours before sailing were memorably spent, Agnes had confirmation of the very different world that was opening up to her.

As we gatecrash the party of family and friends at The Imperial that gave the amateurs such a good send-off that evening, we find no sign of the seven professionals, for they had all signed up earlier in the afternoon and then moved on to their own accommodation. Agnes understood cricket's class distinctions, and for the moment kept to herself the irony that there were some professionals in the party, like Lillywhite and Southerton, who seemed to conduct themselves with more propriety and decorum than some amateurs, her Gilbert included. As for her new brother-in-law Fred, he was making enough noise that evening to be heard back in Bristol as he danced a lurid galop, egged on by cousin Wally Gilbert, with several red-faced young Surrey amateurs in his train – Augustus Oelrichs, Charles Burls, and the amiable new county secretary at The Oval, an influential journalist whom her dear Gilbert should clearly cultivate, Charles Alcock. Gilbert, she was pleased to note, had been behaving with the kind of dignity she had sought to instil in him in a gentle pep talk, though it had to be said that since the arrival of Frizzy Bush's large party, Gilbert's best intentions had slipped a little . . .

Martha was the focus of a large discussion group, predominantly female. It was helpful for Agnes to listen to Gilbert's mother talking so proudly about him and giving away how much she had spoilt him over the years. If Agnes was going to be successful in managing her dear giant, toning down his excesses and drawing out of him the very best, she needed all the ideas she could muster. Martha's power to dominate was notable. So, too, her unwillingness to give way to advancing years. Now that she had thrown away her widow's weeds, she was again indulging her liking for colourfully flamboyant dress, plump though she was.

Martha's sister Rose sat happily beside her. Rose had come down from Great Malvern, where she was running a small school for girls, to see off her son, Wally Gilbert. Agnes looked forward to getting to know him. He was just three years her senior, but (like W.G. himself) her second uncle. There had once been a famous soldier of the same name serving in India, so Wally had found himself being called 'The Colonel' and the strangely inappropriate nickname had stuck. Wally had been living at The Chesnuts as he qualified residentially for Gloucestershire, and he and Fred had become quite as outrageous as Fred and Billy Pocock.

Rose and her brother, Uncle Alfred, were soon reminiscing about the good old days and the work they had done together in Bristol; the lovely scenes that Rose, a talented artist, had drawn onto stone to be turned into beautiful lithographs through Alfred's expertise; and the finely illustrated books they had produced during that golden period. Rose was less keen to discuss with Agnes the sadness and complications involving a second marriage that had frustrated her artistic talents and consigned her to a life of genteel drudgery. She was reticent, too, about her present husband George Mowbray Gilbert, Wally Gilbert's father, who had once run Goodenough House, the school at Ealing where E.M. had been a pupil and where Wally himself had been born. Uncle Alfred reminisced somewhat carefully about the disastrous period when, with George Mowbray as his partner, he had revived and marketed his father's kite-powered '*charvolants*'. Rose's second husband was now living in retirement at the school she was running. He had not come down to Southampton. Money was tight.

Much of the conversation at the Imperial was naturally about the fifty-two-day voyage and the P. & O. liner, the *Mirzapore*, that was to take them as far as Ceylon. Said to be the very latest in wind-assisted steamers and only launched two years earlier, it had drawn much attention, at a distance, that afternoon with its tall funnel and three towering masts. Compared to later liners like the *Titanic*, it was of course very small, under half the length and width. But it was of a similar size to E.M.'s *Great Britain*, just a little narrower and not much longer.

The reality of the social divide in the touring party was carefully blurred in W.G.'s *Reminiscences*. The reader is left to imagine that the professionals were with the amateurs at the Imperial Hotel: 'We were a merry party at dinner that evening, though some of the team did not like the idea of leaving England for the first time'. Likewise, the bland comment that 'some of the team were good sailors and some were bad' glosses over the distinction between W.G.'s party, among the hundred and forty first-class passengers, and the seven professionals enduring severe second-class discomfort with thirty others. There were two separate groups travelling to Australia. Understandable resentment resulted.

* * *

The next morning there was a crisis. The captain of the *Mirzapore*, momentarily bridging the amateur-professional divide, entertained the whole team, their families and friends to a farewell breakfast on board ship. The unreliable Harry Jupp, however, had failed to make the tug that took them out to it and, when breakfast was over and all farewells spoken, there was still no sign of him. Charles Alcock, who, as Surrey's secretary, knew all about Jupp's potential for disaster, headed off on a frantic, last-minute search. By the time Jupp was found, the ship had cast off from its mooring. Alcock, however, bundled the heavily hung-over Surrey batsman into a mail tug and somehow both Jupp and the post were hoisted aboard. Though Brownlee had fun with the incident, W.G. was furious. The episode was passed over in stony silence in *Reminiscences*.

* * *

When at last they began to find their sea legs, Agnes and W.G. looked on with amused pleasure as romances blossomed, particularly at formal events under warm night skies: 'There was witching moonlight,' wrote Brownlee, 'and music, dancing and quiet walking and talking with the fair sex became prevalent...' But sometimes things were less lyrical. Brownlee also wrote of an occasion when a Scotsman, bested in love one particular evening, retired to his cabin and began playing his bagpipes so loudly that 'it was more than human nature could bear'. One of the amateurs who was 'always ready to take up the cause of the fair' led a group of giggling young people to the Scotsman's cabin and poured the contents of a large water jug through an open porthole over him. The drenched Scot, catching sight of Fred leading the laughter, cried out, 'Mr Grace, you are no gentleman!' When Fred told him 'to apologise or take a thrashing', he quickly apologised.

* * *

They reached Melbourne mid-December. Victoria's capital was a boom city with a get-rich-quick culture fanned by the gold rush. It had magnificent new buildings in the centre and a mass of shanties on the outskirts. A rough, winner-takes-all atmosphere prevailed. Fortunes were being made and lost. Gambling was endemic.

The tour itself had sinister undertones. W.G.'s high demands, turned down by the Melbourne cricket establishment the year before, had been taken up by a somewhat shady syndicate. Fred later wrote, 'It was most unfortunate for the team that they should have fallen into the hands of twelve speculators who knew little of cricket'. This not particularly generous overview still helpfully points us in the direction of the tortured figure who masterminded and managed the whole frantic tour, a Melbourne entrepreneur called William Biddle.

Biddle knew rather more about the game than G.F. suggested. He had been secretary for a while of the Melbourne Cricket Club, and in that capacity had given the leading speech of welcome to George Parr and his team on their first arrival. Married with a young family and a house in what was currently one of Melbourne's most exclusive areas, St Kilda, he seemed the epitome of prosperity. His conduct, too, during his management of the tour, appeared at all times 'genial, frank and manly'.

But Biddle was an archetypal speculator. He had come to Australia in the gold rush, after earlier having tried his luck in California. He even had a small shanty town on the west coast of America named Biddleville after him. In Melbourne Biddle had attempted to put his past experiences in mining to good use, and, at the same time, had gone into what seemed a prospering wine business. Unfortunately instead of making him good money it went into hasty liquidation. He was also defrauded by a partner in his gold-mining company at Gaffney's Creek at about the same time that he had persuaded the Melbourne Cricket Club to appoint him chief negotiator of the English Cricketers' Committee trying to land a deal with W.G. When the three leading Melbourne clubs withdrew at W.G.'s first request for £1,500, Biddle gratefully seized on the gamble of leading the whole speculation himself.

The word must have been out in Melbourne that Biddle had his own somewhat questionable agenda, for at the team's very first lunch reception at the Melbourne Town Hall the Mayor, in thanking the promoters for the undertaking, had added, 'though I can't be sure whether it is for the good of cricket or a money speculation'. 'For the good of cricket!' cried Biddle crisply. 'On the other hand,' he added with a modest smile, 'We wouldn't, of course, object to its paying...'

The Graces' first days in Melbourne passed off with little hint of the crises simmering just beneath the surface. It was thrilling for Agnes to be driven with Gilbert round the packed South Melbourne ground as guests at a cricket cup match final and to be fêted as celebrities. West Brompton suddenly seemed a long way away. The Melbourne mood, however, changed suddenly shortly afterwards and she had a difficult job keeping Gilbert calm at the Melbourne Cricket Club's ground during the first match of the tour, against an Eighteen of Victoria. Unfortunately it had begun on Boxing Day with most of the team dreadfully hung-over. There was also a frightening accident en route to the ground on the second day's play, when Fred had insisted on driving their carriage and had applied so much whip that the horse had bolted and the carriage overturned. These setbacks, however, were minor in comparison to an absolutely humiliating innings defeat.

Despite the inglorious result, Agnes had enjoyed herself. How marvellous it was for the new bride to watch her husband scoring 33 and an undefeated 51; to see all the ladies wincing and screaming as one of his hits descended towards them; to hear the ovation when he sent the ball right out of the ground and smashing into the white fence beyond; to have her Gilbert's regal batting matched by Melbourne's quite princely entertaining; to lunch in that huge marquee, the two of them together in the midst of all the VIPs; and, joy upon joy, to have no less a person than the Governor's wife saying charming things about her new hat.

But there was no placating Gilbert over the whispers that the All-England Eleven had thrown the match for money; that it was 'a bookmakers' team'. Had Gilbert actually been on the telegraph at the ground, warning friends in England to lay off their bets as the match was going to be lost? She couldn't believe so. She felt sorry, too, for the delightfully gentle Ferrington Holker Boult who, poor man, had been roundly condemned in his umpiring for failing to give Gilbert out when he had snicked the ball to the wicket-keeper. She had to admit that she, too, had heard the snick. Indeed everybody in the southern hemisphere must have done. But didn't they realise that Ferry had done the right thing? There was a huge crowd – 40,000 over the three days – and the entrance fee of two shillings and sixpence was exorbitant. How could they be so unpleasant to Ferry when so very rightly he was giving the spectators value for their money?

The professionals were less happy in Melbourne than Agnes, consigned as they were to the run-of-the-mill White Hart and hearing that the amateurs were living it up at the costly Port Phillip Club Hotel in Flinders Street. (Fortunately they didn't know that William Biddle, in trying to cope with W.G.'s lavish expectations, was making other last-minute economies in their direction.) The Graces also spent time at Charterisville, in the exclusive Heidelberg Hills outside the city, as guests of David Charteris McArthur, a former captain of Melbourne Cricket Club and then its president. McArthur, who had given Biddle his make-or-break opportunity, had emigrated with his wife from Scotland on his appointment as a young man to the Bank of Australasia. He was now in his mid-sixties, living on the huge estate that he himself had created, the leader of a group of Melbourne bankers who had never had it so good. W.G. found Charterisville marvellously situated for three of his most dearly loved and passionately pursued relaxations: hunting, shooting and fishing. 'Even the goldfish in Mr McArthur's lake,' noted Brownlee mischievously, 'were not free from Grace's marauding instincts.'

Agnes, who was not a country girl, struggled to accept the widespread slaughter of animals that accompanied her husband's progress around Australia, but she nonetheless was his cheerful companion on New Year's Eve as they set out to Ballarat on a journey of over 100 miles involving tedious changes of train. The sweltering heat was hard to bear, but she was fascinated by the flourishing mining industry in this boom town, twenty-five years on from the first gold rush, and they visited several mines during the visit.

In front of a crowd of over 15,000, W.G. and G.F. excelled with a century apiece and the tourists scored a massive 470. 'The wicket played beautifully,' commented a local paper, 'the sun shone hotly; they scored tremendously; we fielded abominably; all drank excessively.' Despite 7-71 from W.G., who was in the process of converting from medium pace to slow, the Twenty-Two of Ballarat held out for a draw.

As soon as the match was over, W.G. and Agnes left for Melbourne, 'accompanied by the remainder of the gentlemen players of the English team'. Such brusque departures often caused offence and this was one such occasion. W.G. was roundly censured. He had, after all, been expensively entertained and given the honour of planting a tree on the ground. The Dutch elm, now over a hundred and forty years old, was recently given a plaque explaining its special pedigree.

The quick escape allowed the couple a day and half together before the first and only parting on the tour, W.G. and his friends returning to Ballarat to begin, by old-fashioned Cobb's Coach, nearly two weeks of lengthy and difficult travel for matches at Stawell and Warrnambool. Meanwhile Agnes, happily relaxing in Melbourne, had a further chance to mix with the McArthurs and hear entertaining stories of Melbourne's earlier days. They had arrived, for example, in a cutter with £3,000, all in coins, with which McArthur was to open the new branch of his bank. They had an armed guard and two fierce bulldogs with them all the way. McArthur was full of memories of early cricket. He had participated in the first match ever played in Australia.

The team's return prefaced a sixteen-hour journey by ship to Sydney, where they played two matches. They also diverted to meet a Bathurst twenty-two. The Graces were entertained lavishly by the Governor of New South Wales, fifty-year-old Hercules Robinson, a jovial Sandhurst-educated Londoner, who thought cricket a wholesome and manly sport, although his primary concern was the turf and his string of outstanding racehorses. W.G. and Agnes delighted in Government House which had been built a few years earlier like a romantic castle, replete with turrets, towers and battlements and beautifully situated alongside the Royal Botanic Gardens, overlooking the future site of the Sydney Opera House. Agnes' opposite number at Government House came from the Irish nobility. The

Hon. Nea Arthur Ada Rose D'Amour was 'a majestic-looking woman', noted for her gaiety and love of society, but Agnes coped well. Any difficult moments were smoothed away by the personable Fred, whose handsome good looks were rumoured to have been the cause why the whole of the Robinson family, their twenty-year-old daughter included, not only supported the matches at Sydney but also travelled up to Bathurst.

Sydney was the current home of Billy Pocock, who delightedly played for the Australians in two games against the tourists, and, in the first of them, vindicated all the hours he had spent in The Chesnuts' net with contributions that enabled the New South Wales Eighteen to win. Fred had the pleasure, however, of bowling his old friend out, and he did so again in the second game, when W.G.'s fine 73 helped All-England to a big victory against a strong Fifteen of New South Wales and Victoria.

History does not relate one word on this reunion of the old Chesnuts tearaways which was likely to have been exhilaratingly wild and not something that the shrewd Agnes would have fiercely resisted. W.G. must later have had great fun in limiting Arthur Porritt, ghosting his autobiography, to tales of exquisitely gentle forays in Sydney, the very antithesis to what might have happened under the aegis of Billy Pocock: 'We were taken in a launch to explore the charming nooks and coves in the Bays . . . and we were enraptured by the exquisite views which were brought under our notice that afternoon. In every respect the picnic was a triumphant success. The arrangements were perfect, the weather faultless, and the means provided for us to amuse ourselves were innumerable.' It would always remain 'a subject for pleasant retrospection'.

History does relate, however, that W.G. did not go down at all well in Sydney and during the second match there he was involved in a public brawl. His antagonist was Bill Runting, secretary of the South Melbourne club which had entertained him and Agnes so graciously on their first arrival in Victoria. Runting, an accountant and real estate agent, would have been in close negotiation with Biddle at the time and was probably all too aware that W.G.'s demands were in the process of ruining his friend. Although he was to become a Vice-President of the Victorian Cricket Association, he embraced the culture of boom or bust and was himself to experience both eventualities. Biddle tried hard to minimise the outrage the Australian press were expressing over W.G.'s behaviour, suggesting the brawl was 'a slight misunderstanding, not worth noting'. But the press were not to be denied. 'The public,' declared the *Bendigo Advertiser* typically, 'has had quite enough of this Mr Grace, who has completely failed to establish his claim to being in any sense of the word a "gentleman" and whose team is beaten by the veriest muffs of the colonial cricket field.'

The press attack made for a hostile atmosphere at Bendigo, which, for better and worse, brought out W.G.'s fighting instincts. 'Standing up fully to everything' on a wicket on which 'the ball got up and caused most of the batsmen to dodge', he impressed with the bravery of his 53 and 72 not out. Unfortunately, as the

Bendigo Advertiser gleefully reported in much detail, he undid all the good work by swearing at the chairman of the local cricket club, suggesting that he was no gentleman and attacking him. Bystanders leapt in quickly to separate them, which was just as well, for on the voyage out on the *Mirzapore*, in what was meant to be a little light sparring with boxing gloves, W.G. had flattened one playmate.

Each crisis formed part of Agnes' steep learning curve. But far from shrinking back from her challenges, she relished them. One little incident shows her at ease in her new life. She was arriving at the Bathurst ground in a carriage full of local VIPs when one of them bet her that W.G. would not hit the ball out of the ground. Betting was hardly the proper thing for a well-brought up English lady, but without a moment's hesitation Agnes won the hearts of all around by smilingly accepting. W.G., of course, did his very best to make sure she won. 'I got hold of one ball full in the bat,' he remembered later, 'and sent it right over the scoring box, but, unfortunately it landed just inside the ground, and so Mrs Grace lost her bet...'

Throughout the tour they were greeted by smiling hosts and honoured with lengthy lunches, dinners and speeches. Conviviality flowed in marquees, country houses and town halls; many ballrooms resounded with waltzes and galops as they danced into the early hours. Tasmania, which they bravely reached after twenty-nine gruelling hours in a ship half the size of the *Mirzapore*, was typical, both matches there being followed by dinner-dances of some opulence. Tasmanian socialising, indeed, was so special that Fred returned there later on, absenting himself from the last match in Australia. Agnes got on splendidly with the small amateur coterie, but regretted that Gilbert regularly missed opportunities for mixing with the professionals and lessening the tensions. On private shooting excursions, for example, he would invariably take The Colonel as his companion, sometimes with Fred and Frizzy. When an *ad hoc* single-wicket match against Ten of Warrnambool was arranged, the team-mates he chose were, of course, Fred, The Colonel and Frizzy.

It was no surprise the tour ended in acrimony. Biddle's embattled situation led to more and more savings on the professionals' expenses. Disgruntled with their second-class lot, they put in for first-class travel home but were refused. So in mid-March 1874 the professionals boycotted a farewell dinner in Melbourne, hosted by the promoters at the Criterion Hotel, Collins Street. Their spokesman, Jim Lillywhite, also wrote an inflammatory letter to the press (as sympathetic to the English professionals as they were hostile to W.G.), carefully laying the blame on Biddle rather than W.G.

* * *

It seems a good dinner to gatecrash. We shan't, of course, see Agnes there, for the majority of such celebratory dinners were all-male affairs, nor shall we see the seven protesting professionals, but, if we free up our imaginations, we shall at least be able to get a glimpse of the struggle William Biddle was having to make money out W.G.

Presiding over the dinner from the top table with W.G. beside him, and with the whole volatile enterprise in the final stages of utter disarray, Biddle was trying hard not to look as desperately miserable as he felt. His speculation had promised so much. Each and every Australian cricket association that wanted to play All-England had had to pay him for the privilege as well as cover the tourists' travel and living expenses. That meant, in theory at least, there was a huge profit to be made, more than enough to save him from ruin. But Grace's personal demands had been overwhelming. And it had been his own fault! He should have gone into the business of the expenses with much more care.

The food was excellent and the finest wines in liberal supply. Biddle tried to simulate enjoyment as he sampled the Lafite's bouquet and smiled around at the other ninety diners. The cost of this Criterion dinner was going to be considerable, but what was one small setback in the face of total catastrophe? Bonhomie, thank goodness, was prevailing in the room. The many resentments between the two sets of cricketers were, for the moment at least, in a state of truce. Not that he had two complete sets. Biddle stared at the seven empty seats. It had been his bad luck that the rift between Grace and his professionals had become so devastatingly bad and so public from the very moment of their arrival. There had been such initial enthusiasm when it was heard that Grace was coming. The nation was ready to go Grace-crazy. But somehow, in the twinkling of an eye, the-hero-we-all-love had become the-villain-we-all-hate. It was hard to sit next to the man, scoffing all the food before him, swilling down the drink and still grumbling about this and that. The man was intolerable. A monster. A hydra with a hundred bearded heads.

The tourists still had one contracted fixture left. Biddle felt a sudden sense of joy at the trick he had played on Grace. The monster had been expecting a match at the Adelaide Oval. But Adelaide thought they could get him cheaply and wouldn't meet Biddle's asking price. So the match in South Australia was going to take place somewhere a little less agreeable. Yorke's Peninsula! Biddle's anxious face eased a little, transforming itself, even, into a pained grin. He raised his glass to a neighbour or two and gulped some more of the nectar down. Yorke's Peninsula! The Kadina Racecourse ground! He'd been able to extract an absolutely huge sum from that prosperous little mining community out in the wilds. Biddle's misery receded considerably at the thought. And there was every chance that the whole of Adelaide would flock in their thousands to the distant racecourse for their only chance of ever watching the controversial Champion. Grace at Kadina! The idea was as preposterous as it was irresistibly funny. Biddle triumphant against the odds! Scooping his part of massive Yorke profits and averting total catastrophe?

It was time for the speeches he had dreaded. The proposing of a toast to 'the All-England Eleven, coupled with the name of Mr W.G. Grace'! All teeth and smiles! But perhaps, after all, he could do it, if he kept thinking of Kadina and ignoring the seven empty places. Yes, it was easy. The platitudes came slipping off his tongue. 'As one of those who was instrumental in inducing Mr Grace to pay us a visit' – and thereby hung a tale – 'I can only express my gratification at the manner in which the venture has been received' – who was he kidding? – 'not only by cricketers but by the public at large...' He found himself positively beaming at the large bearded man beside him who had done his best to destroy him. 'Yes, deep gratification, gentlemen.' He sat down to huge applause, and the image of Kadina loomed large.

He knew that Grace in his response would express innocent surprise at the empty places. He did! He'd then go on to complain about the umpiring. Spot on! And whinge about the press. Bull's eye! Biddle's mounting desire to counter the Grace rudeness with hysterical laughter was only stopped as the large bearded man beside him unexpectedly bent right down to raise a glass under his very nose and declare, 'My stay has been a very pleasant one. I only regret it has not been a little longer.' A little longer! Biddle's mind boggled and mouth dropped open at the sheer thought of it. Then he heard the tills of Yorke Peninsula calling out to him in unison, and he smiled modestly at the sight of all the raised glasses and all the pink, smiling faces.

The rest of the evening passed off in a haze. Biddle was vaguely aware of hostilities breaking out at last between the Victorians and Englishmen. He likewise heard, at a great distance, Grace's younger brother, who had recently tried to cheat the umpire when in the field at Melbourne, now having the effrontery to pretend he hadn't: 'People here set up being judges of cricket, who know nothing about it! When I stopped that ball with my foot, everyone cried out "Four"! In England the umpire always asks the person if he has stopped the ball, and when a gentleman gives his word it is always relied on! It was a LIE that the ball was stopped by a tuft of grass – a downright LIE!' The louder the young man shouted, the more Biddle felt an overwhelming urge to go to sleep, to erase the whole hideous memory of the arrogant Graces. To erase, too, the further complaints now coming, predictably, from the Grace coterie: the large Bush, the small Gilbert and even the flimsy Ferrington Boult. ('I'm not a good umpire and I don't pretend to be, BUT...') All equally critical. And now the Hydra, holding forth again in that irritatingly high-pitched voice. 'The papers said that I used very insulting language to Mr Budd, the umpire. This I did NOT do and NEVER had the slightest intention of doing!' With an effort Biddle gathered together his failing capacities. It was important to end the evening positively; to pretend to Grace that he was set for a good time at Yorke's Peninsula; and to reiterate – this was really crucial – that he should decline *any* overtures from Adelaide to play an extra match there. He'd signed a contract to that effect. It was absolutely crucial that he kept to it. A share of a big payout at Yorke's Peninsula, with the people of Adelaide all going to the racecourse, might not necessarily save him from disaster, but it was certainly his last chance . . .

* * *

W.G., however, when approached by Adelaide, at once let it be known that he was indeed very interested in a further fixture there. Biddle's ruin was complete. Desperate, he took legal action, but failed. The Adelaide public duly stayed at home for the Kadina game. W.G.'s extra match at the Adelaide Oval went ahead, and as his eleven had fulfilled its contracted fixtures, he was able to pocket the considerable sum he demanded for it.

Agnes watched helplessly as the final six days in South Australia unfolded grimly. Harry Jupp's period in a padded cell after a terrifying attack of the DTs summed it all up. She would not soon forget the disarray of the abrupt departure from Kadina for Adelaide. Nor the swift and bad-tempered departure from there with the absurdity of hiding on their ship at Glenelg the day before it actually departed. The ill-feeling Gilbert was leaving behind him after so much Australian goodwill and hospitality was heart-breaking.

For William Biddle there were no more speculative dice to be thrown. Like the Melbourne Club's star cricketer Richard Wardell, who had jumped to his death in the Yarra River only months before the arrival there of the *Mirzapore*, Biddle knew he was totally finished. Overcome by his debts, he met a sudden, welcome end only months after the tourists left Glenelg.

* * *

From a purely cricketing point of view, W.G. could claim with justification that, after a poor start, things had gone well. Ten of the fifteen matches had been won. He topped his team's batting averages, though his 39 was quite closely followed by Fred's 33, and Fred achieved the highest innings of the tour (154). Lillywhite and Southerton had bowled by far the most overs, taking 174 and 146 wickets respectively at around 5 each, but W.G.'s 65 were at a satisfactory average of 7. His unspectacular statistics reflected his many off-field preoccupations, not least the new experience of having to consider someone else's welfare in addition to his own.

As a twenty-year-old bride suddenly asked to cross the world and immerse herself in an all-male sport, Agnes had performed superbly. W.G. had likewise done well as a husband, showing sympathy and thoughtfulness. When match situations allowed, he had escorted Agnes between the grounds and their hotel, for she did not always sit through the entire day's play. Whenever possible, he had made alternative travel arrangements on her behalf, to avoid early mornings or late nights. When they finally returned to England and docked at Southampton on 18 May 1874, she was six months' pregnant.

* * *

A day later, Martha was holding a homecoming party for her two sons, nephew and new daughter-in-law. There was so much cricket to talk about! So many additions to be made to her scrapbook! There was also a special surprise for them – a family get-together three days hence over at Thornbury, arranged by Teddy, including a match with Clifton. He'd specially reserved three places for them in his team, knowing how much they'd like to play on the new ground he'd been developing at Alveston, alongside The Ship, that splendid old coaching inn. There'd be marquees, a band, and a wonderful gathering of the whole clan. Alfred would be coming over from Chipping Sodbury, Henry from Kingswood Hill.

* * *

The Thornbury Cricket Club still plays at Alveston, though the small and rough country ground over which E.M. had laboured, assiduously rolling the wicket and ensuring the sheep munched away at the outfield, is hard to equate with today's extensive and beautifully manicured version, servicing a vibrant club that fields many adult and youth elevens. The Ship, where for years the teams used to change, as well as eat, drink and have fun, is likewise flourishing and full of old oak beams, open fires and flagstone floors with which the Graces would have felt familiar. The only disappointment is that in the 1960s, after a Trust House takeover, an elongated one-storey hotel was put up (today under Premier Inn ownership) physically separating the ground from the adjacent pub.

The club has a splendid memento of the two brothers in its main pavilion, reminding everyone that E.M. was captain, secretary and treasurer from 1871 to 1910, with 64 Thornbury centuries to his credit and a top score of 327 not out; and that W.G., 'probably the most famous cricketer in the world', played in fifty-one matches on the ground in 1874–98, making 3,519 runs and taking 194 wickets.

The first of W.G.'s fifty-one matches at Thornbury, on his homecoming from Australia, proved suitably memorable. Clifton were swiftly dispatched by W.G. and E.M. W.G. thereupon amassed 259 in less than three hours, entertaining Agnes and the family with ten sixes. Fred likewise hit a lightning 123 in a stand with his brother of 288.

The Graces were home. A new season had begun. Martha, on Uncle Alfred's arm, proudly bestrode the Thornbury ground in her brightest dress. If Agnes had any slight anxieties, she kept them sensibly to herself. Martha might be a challenging proposition at the moment, but she could bide her time.

7

A Lesson for Grimsby

On a pedestal above the rest, 1874–76

Two months later, at close of play on 6 July 1874, a large, bearded figure was seen jumping into a horse-drawn cab outside Lord's, where he had just played a breezy knock for the Gents v. Players. Not long afterwards, as the vehicle drew up before 19 Coleherne Road, he was leaping clear, racing up the steps and pounding on the door. Inside, there was wonderful news. Jereboams were in order. William Gilbert Grace junior had been born. The long-awaited Bertie!

Over the next few weeks W.G. remained in wildly celebratory mood, his 153 for the United South in Dublin and 167 for Gloucestershire at Yorkshire's Bramall Lane being among four exhilarating centuries. The proud father naturally topped the national averages in 1874 and, though the following season of 1875 was a wet, low-scoring one, he was still 'superior to any batsman' and 'on a pedestal above the rest of his fellows,' the first cricketer ever to achieve a first-class double, with 1,498 runs and 191 wickets. On the firmer wickets of 1876 he enjoyed a truly special season that was quickly dubbed an *annus mirabilis*, an all-round triumph with 2,622 first-class runs (at over 62 per innings), 130 wickets and (for the sixth successive year) more catches than anyone else. Unsurprisingly, Gloucestershire were the winners of the unofficial county championship. *Lillywhite's Annual* likened W.G. to the legendary eighteenth-century racehorse Eclipse, always coming first, the rest nowhere. 'For the last ten years Mr W.G. Grace has stood alone as the most marvellous cricketer of his time.'

This outstandingly successful period coincided with an important domestic change, signalled by the birth of Bertie in London rather than Bristol. Agnes had put her foot down. She decided to have her baby at her parents' home in London instead of The Chesnuts. She likewise struck a bargain with Gilbert. He recommenced (at least, in theory) his medical studies, signing up at St Bart's, and Aunt Caroline masterminded a flat for them in Earls Court. To keep Martha happy, they stayed at The Chesnuts every August, the month when the county played their home matches at the colleges of Clifton and Cheltenham.

* * *

In one such August, in 1876, W.G. was persuaded by *The World* to participate in a series of articles featuring 'Celebrities at Home'. 'W.G. Grace at Downend', however, offers no insights into the new domestic arrangements. As was his way, he met the journalist's every ball with a straight, defensive bat. The usual generalities resulted:

A black-haired, black-browed, black-bearded giant, with a good-humoured twinkle in his hazel eye, and a rich musical Gloucestershire ring in his voice, Mr. W.G. Grace is a standing – a six-feet-two standing – illustration of the good old sporting verity, that a good big one is better than a good little one – that quality being equal, length, strength and weight will tell. As he rises from his chair to welcome us, we become sensible of the colossal proportions of the famous cricketer, who when in the field never looks so tall as he really is. Perhaps his tremendous shoulders and long muscular arms bring down his height, but it is certain that in the open air he never 'looks his inches', save perhaps in the orchard which surrounds his mother's house at Downend.

More revealing was the elevated company he was keeping when a compilation of *The World's* interviews was later published in book form. Among the accompanying essays were 'H.R.H. the Prince of Wales at Sandringham', 'Mr Tennyson at Haslemere', 'Mr Gladstone at Hawarden', 'Mr Henry Irving in Bond Street', 'The Earl of Beaconsfield at Hughenden', 'The Marquis of Salisbury at Hatfield', 'Sir Rowland Hill at Hampstead' and 'Dr John Henry Newman at Birmingham'. W.G., the single sporting celebrity, was sandwiched between Gustave Doré and the Duke of Beaufort.

* * *

In becoming a national hero, W.G. transcended class barriers, breaking free of the game's upper-class establishment and his own middle-class Pocock roots. His involvement throughout the 1870s with the United South had something to do with this. His travels were relentless. In the *annus mirabilis* of 1876 his first-class matches consisted of eight games for Gloucestershire, nine for M.C.C. and various teams of Gentlemen, and five for the South against the North. In addition, however, he turned out in sixteen three-day games for the United South, going all over the country, from Dublin to Huddersfield, from Hull to Glossop – wherever there was the prospect of a decent pay packet. His United South commitments accounted for the best part of two months of each season, and it helped develop his image as the people's champion, always accessible, travelling in their trains, hiring their cabs, staying in their hotels and enjoying their recreation grounds, as he ubiquitously promoted both himself and the game.

It was while he was fulfilling one such United South commitment, in mid-July 1876, that he made the biggest score of his entire career. He was playing against the Twenty-two of Grimsby and District. It was a one-off, the only match he ever played at Grimsby, and such an unusually memorable game that we must go there to see it for ourselves.

* * *

First stop is The Yarborough, a Wetherspoon pub in Bethlehem Street, one of those large hotels the pragmatic Victorians built alongside their new railway stations. There is currently a splendid project afoot to restore its third storey to hotel use, good news for all those travelling in the steps of W.G., for it was at The Yarborough Hotel, built in 1851, that W.G. stayed for the three-day Grimsby fixture, accompanied by his two devoted acolytes, brother Fred and cousin Wally Gilbert.

With its striking appearance of red and white (bricks offset with ashlar dressings) and its elaborate Italianate style, the solidly proportioned Yarborough was exactly the kind of imposing and sophisticated mid-Victorian creation that was so hated by the brutalist architectural gurus of the 1960s. It was duly assigned for demolition, but the ghost of W.G. must have intervened – the building is said to be haunted – and at the last minute it was saved. Today, thank goodness, it boasts a Grade II listing.

W.G. arrived at The Yarborough in fine spirits. His 169 for Gentlemen v. Players at Lord's was still on everyone's lips and so, too, the nineteen wickets he had taken in that match and the return fixture at Prince's. He was also excited that he would shortly become a father again.

Grimsby and District were hosting the United South on the Worsley Cricket Club ground, which disappeared under housing development as long ago as the early 1880s. With an old map to hand, we are heading off from The Yarborough to the former Ainslie Street cemetery, now a small park. At its far end, Peaks Parkway (the busy A16) runs along what was in W.G.'s time the East Lincolnshire railway line. Worsley Cricket Club's ground lay immediately beyond. Willingham Street now bisects it. Hainton Avenue, where the ground had its entrance, marks its furthest extent. It was not far from The Yarborough. W.G. and his two henchmen would have arrived there by cab in about five minutes.

It was an attractive and spacious ground. Its pretty pavilion had its own fenced enclosure and a tiny first-floor eyrie that gave the scorers a good view. The railway line that bounded the western side was protected by greenery. Though a gas works dominated the northern boundary, enough tents and marquees had been erected to create an air of festivity which the Railway Servants' Brass Band toiled long and hard to sustain.

W.G. was not in the best of tempers when he met his opposite number, the Revd Charles Warren, captaining Grimsby's twenty-two. Infuriatingly, the United South were short of three players who had missed their train and were not expected for some time. Then there was the awful state of the outfield. The grass had only been cut on the pitch and its immediate surroundings, so the ball was going to stop dead everywhere else.

Charles Warren, however, was even more upset. A curate running a mission hall near the Grimsby docks, he was a man of passionate feelings, a thirty-two-year-old devoted to the cause of fighting the sloth and despair he so often detected in his needy parishioners. He could be a tigerish individual, and he was feeling distinctly tigerish at the moment towards Worsley's professional, the easy-going Jack May, whose job it was to have the ground in tip-top shape. Quite how he had managed to let the grass on the outfield reach its current state was hard to imagine. But it was typical of slothful Jack. Only a few weeks ago they'd had a set-to over the Worsley net, which May, as the ground bowler, was also meant to look after. Having a quick batting practice one afternoon, Warren had been peppered by blows to the body from May's usually innocuous medium-pacers that an unrolled surface had made venomous. Warren had sorted out that piece of laziness by insisting May have a bat and then bowling fast bodyline until he howled for mercy. But clearly slothful Jack had gone back to his old, old ways.

The Revd Warren set high standards and expected them from others. A former Cambridge University Blue who was never without his light blue cap, a symbol of attainment to which all should aspire, he was acknowledged as 'the finest cricketer that ever donned flannels in this district'. Educated at Oakham, he had briefly been a member of the famous Cambridgeshire side of the 1860s, scoring good runs in teams that included the famous Tom Hayward* and Robert Carpenter, but the call to the church had ended his promising career early.

He had first come across W.G. ten years earlier when playing against him for the North v. the South at Lord's. W.G. could only have been eighteen at the time, but he had been too pleased with his abilities to endear himself to Warren. And whereas Warren had given up the chance of further cricket glory for his religious calling, W.G. would seem to have put the cricket first and everything else second.

Warren had already had some furious complaints on the morning of the match from Jabez North, the landlord of the (no longer extant) Greyhound Inn, along Victoria Street. As the Worsley club's secretary, North had put up the £100 needed to bring W.G. to Grimsby, though several of the more affluent members, Warren himself included, had contributed their guineas. Jabez needed to fill the ground for three days to make a small profit and had been appalled to discover there were only three well-known players among the eight that had so far deigned to turn up. The United South seemed largely a team of old has-beens! He had been promised players like Pooley, Jupp and Humphrey. But they hadn't come. And in their place the cunning Grace had brought up relatives with the same names. He would fool nobody!

The long tirade over, the Grimsby skipper tigerishly adjusted his Cambridge cap to its severest angle and assured The Greyhound's popular landlord that he would,

---

* Uncle of Surrey's Tom Hayward.

of course, as a matter of principle, raise all these understandable complaints in the proper quarter. Inside the pavilion, W.G. found himself suddenly confronted by a faded light blue cap and a hostile curate. He listened quite patiently at first – Agnes would have been proud of him – as Warren outlined in his clipped, authoritative tones a summary of Jabez North's grievances. W.G. began counting to ten, as recently encouraged to do, until, at only seven, he found himself on a fierce counter-attack. Yes, he had to agree, there had been a problem in getting a good team together, for there were so many conflicting county fixtures these days, and, yes, perhaps it was disappointing that people like Lillywhite, Charlwood and Southerton weren't able to be playing, but no, definitely no, it was not true that his team were a collection of has-beens, and as for the suggestion that he had played a con trick in bringing up two cousins and a brother of Pooley, Jupp and Humphrey with nothing but the same surnames to recommend them, well, all he could say was that, if he weren't speaking to a man of the cloth, he would be responding with considerably more vigour. He relaxed his grip on Warren's shirt collar to emphasise his point.

Charles Warren, who fought to save souls in the backstreets of the docks, was not lightly intimidated and pointed out with similar asperity that no-one in Grimsby, no-one in Cleethorpes, nay, no-one in the whole of the county of Lincolnshire had ever have heard of these alternative Pooleys, Jupps and Humphreys that the United South had brought with them. The game's promoter had every reason to be unhappy.

W.G. had only counted as far as two when he let it be known that he had never been so insulted in his entire life; that any team that contained himself, his brother and his cousin was good enough to take on any opposition the Reverend would care to name; and that here he was, in a forsaken outpost of the British Isles with the constant smell of fish that even the chilly blasts off the Humber couldn't sweep away, when back in London, his dear, dear wife was in the throes of childbirth, something he had completely ignored in the cause of bringing up a fine team to meet with the twenty-two of Grimsby.

Only minutes later, the toss was conducted in tight-lipped monosyllables. W.G. called correctly and announced stiffly to his recalcitrant opposite number that he would bat first. Fielding was out of the question. He would have had to grovel for subs.

The twenty-two of Grimsby and District strode out from the pavilion determinedly, uplifted as always by the sight of Cambridge blue. They were, after all, as Jabez North had jokingly suggested, only playing the Depleted South, those eight who had been sober enough to catch the right train, and, from the grumpy faces of some of them, if they ever actually became an Eleven later in the day, they would probably be no more than a Moderately United South.

The ground was filling encouragingly as W.G. came out to bat with Tom Humphrey, an old Surrey pro, good in his day but not far off fifty and already suffering from a mortal lung complaint. Humphrey's many opening partnerships with Harry Jupp dated back to the 1860s, but in some ways W.G. looked like the older player, for he was striding out with pair of leg-guards tanned dark yellow. Warren might flaunt his Cambridge cap. But what was that compared with the pads that had once belonged to the great Alfred Mynn?

A legend has arisen that W.G. was bowled on the very first ball but stayed at the wicket, blaming the wind for the loss of his bails. It is a good story but untrue, rejected in later years by several Grimsby players. W.G. did, however, survive a perilous moment when only 6. A young fast bowler, John Senescall, who was to play a few matches for Sussex, appealed confidently for lbw, and was loudly supported by many of the twenty-two. The United South's umpire Bill Mortlock resolutely turned the appeal down, but later in the pub confessed his error. 'I did it all for the best, gentlemen! The South had such a bad team that I thought it inadvisable to give W.G. out so early in the game!' This was not the motive, however, that the Revd Warren remembered (when quoted by a friend, Canon Tatham, in the *Memorial Biography* nearly forty years later): 'The umpire was afraid to give him out. Simple as that.'

W.G., who, of course, had paid no attention at all to such an absurd and frivolous appeal, was already planning ahead. He would prove to the landlord of the Greyhound that no United South eleven captained by himself was ever anything but a formidable proposition; he would likewise keep that faded Cambridge cap out in the sunshine, fading even further, as its owner was taught a lesson that he would not swiftly forget, whether in Grimsby, Cleethorpes or in any other part of the county of Lincolnshire. The ball might be stopping dead in the outfield, but he would not to be coerced into lifting his head and taking the dangerous high route. He would play straight and accumulate. They might have twenty-two men in the field, but gaps would always present themselves. A plethora of fielders had never worried him. As his dear father used to say, 'Have patience, my boy, have patience.'

By lunch, when the remainder of his team turned up somewhat sheepishly, he was not only showing patience but timing the ball very sweetly, and there was a thoughtful, less aggressive look beneath that Cambridge cap. It became even more thoughtful as the afternoon unfolded. W.G. had lost a couple of partners. Humphrey had fallen for 22, and an old Hampshire pro, Harry Holmes, had been umpired out by Mortlock's opposite number. But Fred had come in to join him and was playing, as instructed, with exaggerated care. The score mounted. The afternoon went slowly by. There were occasional cries from the Grimsby skipper of 'Come on, you fellows,' but more in hope than expectation. The luxuriant outfield was still eschewed in favour of stolen singles. One of the Grimsby fielders, Bob Lincoln, consigned all day to field in the deep because of his good turn of speed, didn't touch the ball once. By the close of play, the tally showed 217-2. The scorers, up in their eyrie, did a quick addition and announced that W.G. now had 136 and G.F. 29.

There was only limited fraternisation between the two teams that first night. The Grace contingent relaxed at The Yarborough. For them a day that had started none too well was ending in some contentment. Meanwhile in nearby pubs disgruntlement simmered. In The Greyhound there was indignation that the match seemed to be going nowhere and prospects of a good crowd on the next two days were receding. In an era when declarations were not within the rules, it was necessary for teams to surrender wickets to open up matches to an exciting conclusion. But from the look on the Graces' resolute faces at the close of play, such altruism was not on the agenda.

There was a subdued air among the Twenty-two of Grimsby as they re-gathered on the Tuesday. Charles Warren urged renewed activity – 'no sloth in the field, you fellows' – but there was a dullness in several eyes that reflected more than a heavy night in The Greyhound. They had spent a whole day bowling at W.G., imperiously batting in the pads of Alfred Mynn. They had run around, chasing after the ball as their captain urged them on from point, sometimes bumping into each other in their eagerness to prevent more than a single, but all in vain. All for nothing. All for that implacable run-machine to be returning to the crease next day on 136 not out.

There was a spring in the steps of the Graces, however, as they pressed on that morning to the strains of the Railway Servants' Brass Band, and both were enjoying themselves as they started lofting the ball to soft landings in distant places. 'No sloth in the field, you fellows!' But the Grimsby twenty-two were looking distinctly slothful and disheartened when play was mercifully interrupted by a telegraph boy rushing onto the field, handing a telegram to W.G. and rushing back again. At the end of the over, with twenty-two pairs of eyes upon him, W.G. extracted the telegram from his pocket, opened it with a flourish and then walked down the wicket to Fred. Sudden light relief! 'To our surprise,' recalled Bob Lincoln, 'he invited us to adjourn and have champagne with him!' So they all trooped off to a marquee, where corks were soon popping merrily. Spirits rose as more and more corks popped. Hearts began to warm. W.G. was all merriment as again and again he asked the company to raise their glasses to his good lady wife who had just given birth to a second son and made him the happiest man in England. The champagne tasted good. Glasses were refilled. The name of 'young Edgar' was bandied around. More toasts were drunk. And when W.G. announced, with a glint in his eye, that this was such a special day for him that he hoped to break a record or two, their hearts, instead of sinking, rose with joy that they were participating in a great occasion, a day for all to remember, a day for their grandchildren. Old Jabez North, though tired after all those sessions in the field, wore such a beaming smile that there could even be free rounds that night. The skipper, too, known for his stern admonitions on the dangers of the demon drink, was taking more than a quiet sip himself. They adjourned for lunch in the best of spirits, and re-emerged in due course onto the field in a positive state of exhilaration. One or two felt just a little dizzy and Charles Warren seemed unconcerned at mislaying his cap.

The mood dramatically changed. In the afternoon the fielders were both slower and happier, W.G. steelier and more acquisitive. With the score at 282-3, Fred was out for 60, caught on the boundary by Jabez North, a moment of triumph that presaged bad news. Wally Gilbert entered briskly, a sturdy twenty-two-year-old with the snub nose of the Graces and a Hitler-esque moustache. The Colonel could be just as punishing a bat as Fred and, with the fielders light-headed, he and W.G. enjoyed a glorious run-feast, W.G. striking several big shots out of the ground. A few chances came and went. W.G., who had been missed behind the wicket on 180, was dropped at slip on 260. At close of play the telegraph was showing 537-3. The Colonel had reached a brilliant century and it was eventually agreed that W.G. had now reached 314.

After two days' cricket, less than half of one team had batted and six of the United South had spent two whole days in the pavilion, yet there was a gloriously convivial evening on the Tuesday shared by both sides at The Yarborough as W.G. insisted that his good Agnes and her young Edgar should be properly toasted. All anger and frustration in the Grimsby ranks had evaporated, replaced by pleasurable awe and the euphoria of participation in something that could become a piece of cricket history. Even slothful Jack May had been forgiven for the long grass. It was, after all, very comfortable to sit on between overs. The Revd Warren was earnestly holding forth – and was that a glass that he had in his hand? – eager to tell everyone that W.G. had been right all along. Backed up by his brother and cousin, he was, indeed, a team in himself, a batting phenomenon unlikely to be seen again. The tunnel-visioned way he had capitalised on his early piece of luck was something very special. They should thank their lucky stars – no, the Almighty – that a batting masterclass was unfolding before their very eyes.

Old Jabez, too, was suggesting that perhaps they had been a little presumptuous, after all, in their criticisms. Maybe their own team was a little less formidable than they had thought. The Revd Warren, of course, was a class player. Enough said. The vice-captain, the Revd Jimmy Young, likewise, had been in the Winchester eleven for three years and only just missed his Blue at Oxford. Jimmy, such a popular curate of St James, was a fine all-rounder, even if W.G. had been making those lobs of his look a little ordinary. Jack May was a willing enough professional most days, but his three years with Hampshire hadn't come to anything. Little Dan MacLean, their second professional, was a competent wicket-keeper – not averse to knocking off the bails with his toe if the umpire wasn't watching – but he had not made it past the Yorkshire Colts. Their third and final professional addition, young Chris Anthony, was unlikely to make it into the big-time. Even with his father umpiring he never seemed to take any wickets. No, if they were honest, they were really nothing more than a pretty good club side. Yes, Sam Haddelsey had become the first local man to score a century on the Worsley ground but he was, first and foremost, a solicitor in his family firm. Jack Gorbutt was an excellent long-stop, but his real excellence lay in his butcher's shop. Joshua Good's left-handed efforts paled into insignificance with his work as a town administrator. The two young naval officers, stationed at Hull on the *Galatea*, really weren't strong cricketers. It had been noticeable how quickly W.G.

identified young Lt. Aitken as the weakest fielder and made capital out of it. Bob Lincoln was a good team player, but his expertise was in the building trade and his ambitions all centred on the founding of a Grimsby Town football club. George Clark was a fine engine driver, yet all that steam had made him a little unreliable in the field. As for the Revd James Loft, the forty-three-year-old vicar of sleepy Healing, well, he would never stay at the wicket as long as he did in the pulpit. The toasts to Agnes and baby Edgar resounded around the Yarborough well into the night. Everyone was agreed. There had been two wonderful days so far, and they were all going to enjoy the third.

Smiling faces, then, came through the Hainton Avenue entrance on the final morning. There was only a modest crowd, but no-one cared any more. What mattered was W.G.'s score. Would he, could he, add to the 314? He soon lost Wally, out for a brilliant 116. Three further wickets quickly fell. But W.G. moved inexorably onwards, finding, for a while, an unexpected partner in Bill Palmer, whose decade on the county fringe at Kent and Surrey was currently drawing to its undistinguished close. At 3.30 engine-driver George Clark, standing on the boundary, only had to close his hands around the ball and W.G.'s long innings would have ended. But the ball was a long time in the air, and, in the end, nerves triumphed. So W.G. moved onwards. When the last wicket eventually fell, at around 4.00 p.m., the tally gave the score as 680.

Bob Lincoln later recalled that he and Sam Haddelsey were the two members of the team nearest the pavilion and the first of several to rush up into the eyrie to see the scorer's figures. W.G. by this time had reached the pavilion and called up to enquire his total. '399', shouted the scorer. 'Oh, make it 400!' cried Sam Haddelsey immediately. 'He jolly well deserves it!' Before anybody could suggest otherwise Bob Lincoln had leant over the scorer and added a single.

W.G.'s 400 not out had taken thirteen and a half hours. Unfortunately the marathon innings had only left Grimsby with an hour and a half's batting, precious little compensation for nearly three days in the field. But the champagne had flowed again in the interval, the toasts to W.G. had been long and hearty, the brass band was gallantly replaying its favourite tunes, and both teams came out determined to make their last session together really enjoyable. The Revd Warren showed all his usual style in scoring an elegant 11 before being stumped by Ted Pooley's brother off W.G. Bob Lincoln was bowled for one by Fred – little recompense for the precious run he had added to the champion's 399. The young solicitor Sam Haddelsey, on whose suggestion that one run had been added, also perished early, caught W.G. bowled G.F., but wicket-keeper Dan MacLean scampered around to great effect and after an exhilarating ninety minutes Grimsby had attained a very honourable 88-11. The all-smiling Jabez North would be standing drinks at The Greyhound.

* * *

There was, alas, no chance of W.G. being there or, indeed, making a quick dash to see baby Edgar. There was a train to catch for Huddersfield. The Revd Warren, who had refound his cap, dignified the leave-taking by also bringing out his varsity jacket. The station whistle blew. The circus was moving on. At ten-to-one next day, W.G. and The Colonel would be striding out to open another United South innings . . .

* * *

The Revd Charles Warren returned to the Grimsby docklands reinvigorated. Any slight misgivings about the quality of the Grimsby attack were quickly silenced by W.G.'s exploits the very next month. In three consecutive innings, against some of the best bowlers in England, the run-machine took 344 off Kent at Canterbury; 177 off Notts at Clifton; and 318 not out off Yorkshire at Cheltenham. It was highly therapeutic for the Reverend Charles to read of W.G. smashing Tom Emmett over square leg and onto the roof of Cheltenham's gymnasium; of sixes crashing into the fashionably dressed crowd in the grandstand; and of the total demoralization of the Yorkshire fielders as W.G. landed another direct hit on the main tent. How much he and the rest of the Grimsby twenty-two could sympathise with Tom Emmett's despairing summary: 'It was Grace before lunch, Grace after lunch, Grace all day.'

8

A Hint of Retirement

Medicine and more Australian dramas, 1877–79

The medical studies in London had not been flourishing. Though Bart's in recent times has had the magnanimity to open a W.G. Grace Ward in its Queen Elizabeth Wing, the two winters there had been largely unproductive. The anxious Agnes sought the advice of Henry, always the most reliable of the Grace brothers, who suggested a move to Westminster Hospital, where the student numbers were considerably smaller and the provision less impersonal. By February 1876, therefore, W.G. was dutifully attending Westminster at least twice a week, and on the conclusion of his superb cricket season of 1876, Agnes took another decisive step to help maintain scholastic focus. With financial assistance from her Aunt Caroline, they rented a large detached house in Acton. This was to be the spacious new base from which he must achieve his long-awaited qualifications.

The house, 1 Leamington Park, is in the northern part of the west London suburb of Acton, standing at the corner of a busy one-way road that brings traffic into Horn Lane (the A4000) from the dual carriageway of Western Avenue (the A40). Built in the 1870s at the lower end of a row of tall houses of bold yellow brick decoratively offset with red and black, it was part of a large middle-class development focused around a new Great Western railway station. Although it has now been converted into a number of flats, externally it is much as the Graces knew it, though the back garden (currently a complete wilderness) was narrowed when Horn Lane was widened. The Graces' Acton was rather more peaceful than today's. The occasional horse and cart might have slowly made its way along rustic Horn Lane. A pony and trap might, every now and then, have paused in Leamington Park. But the pace of life there was essentially very gentle – ideal, indeed, for scholastic endeavour.

The four-storeyed house offered a lifestyle more in keeping with W.G.'s national celebrity than the Earls Court flat. There was plenty of space on the top floor for a cook, a lady's maid, a nurse for Edgar and a governess for Bertie. Martha liked it, for she could stay there every time she came up by train to see her grandsons and visit Lord's and Prince's. There was space, too, for Aunt Caroline and Uncle John, who, for the rest of their lives, now moved in with Agnes and W.G.

* * *

Acton proved a good base for the season of 1877 in which W.G. was both the leading batsman and the most effective bowler, backing up nearly 1,500 runs at an average of almost 40 with 179 wickets, and being equally successful in minor matches with the United South. The family's summer holiday in Bristol that year witnessed the three Graces gloriously leading Gloucestershire to another unofficial county championship. At Clifton the whole clan delightedly applauded the defeats of Yorkshire (W.G. 71 and 5-31 and E.M. 53 not out), Sussex (W.G. 6-58 and 5-62 and E.M. 60) and Surrey (W.G. 5-26). There was also a trip to Cheltenham to see the conquest of Notts (W.G. 9-55 and 8-34 and G.F. 83). The public, however, was shocked to learn that this had been W.G.'s swan-song. 'He will no longer be able to devote the summer months to cricket,' *Lillywhite's Companion* declared unequivocally. 'We shall much regret the loss of his grand displays of batting.'

Suggestions of his possible retirement had also spread earlier that year when the Duke of Beaufort, as President of M.C.C., initiated the idea of a National Testimonial, to recognise W.G.'s 'great services to cricket' and 'extraordinary play' and to buy the famous medical student, then approaching thirty, a suitable doctor's practice. The initiative naturally aroused much controversy – whatever skilful words were used to wrap it up, this was an endorsement of shamateurism promulgated by the highest figure in cricket's ruling body – but, with another Gloucestershire ally, Lord Fitzhardinge, succeeding Beaufort as the club's president in 1878, the idea, however controversial, went ahead. Every cricket club in the country was approached for donations. M.C.C. led the way with 100 guineas. The Prince of Wales was a notable contributor.

The only drawback in an otherwise delightful scheme was the way it had thrust the topic of W.G.'s exams uncomfortably into the public spotlight. He was still not making auspicious progress. Moreover, contrary to the mysterious announcements about his impending retirement from the game, he had absolutely no intention at all of letting impending exams deprive the nation of his 'grand displays of batting'.

Agnes, who was again pregnant, made another bid that winter to move Gilbert's studies forward, abetted by brother-in-law Henry, equally determined to save Gilbert from the public humiliation that exam failure could bring. Henry and his wife Leeana lived in a large house in the centre of Bristol's Kingswood Hill. Somewhat misleadingly known as 'The Cottage', it had ample room for Gilbert and his family. They could stay at Kingswood in 1878 for as long as was necessary. Henry himself would personally supervise Gilbert's final revision to ensure no slip-ups. Meanwhile, Aunt Caroline and Uncle John would look after 1 Leamington Park and care for little Bertie and Edgar whenever helpful. They clinched Gilbert's approval with the concession that, if he worked hard at all other times, he need not surrender the cricket season of 1878.

* * *

Kingswood Hill, on the eastern outskirts of Bristol only a few miles south of Mangotsfield, was a busy working-class district. Henry Grace's home and surgery were at Richmond Place, on the corner of Downend Road and Regent Street, but they have not survived, knocked down for a cinema complex that in turn gave way in the 1970s to the Kings Chase Shopping Centre. One tiny memento survives. Built into one of several concrete seats between the shops and a bus shelter is a stone from Richmond Place that once advertised 'Mr Grace's Surgery'. Likewise, his medical practice still continues, situated across the road in modern premises in Macdonald Walk. Now known as The Orchard Medical Centre, it proudly acknowledges W.G.s eldest brother as its founder. No-one could be more appropriately commemorated than Henry Grace, a larger-than-life, no-nonsense character, full of fun and extremely popular. As the inscription on his grave at Downend's Christ Church was later to state, he was 'a truly unselfish man, deservedly beloved'.

* * *

In 1878, a season of damp wickets and low scores, W.G. cut down on his games for the United South but still managed to fit in twenty-four first-class matches, coming third in the national averages with a comparatively modest 28 but also taking 152 wickets. There were three matches of particular note against the touring Australians. The shrewd Jim Lillywhite was behind this historic visit. Two years earlier he had beaten off a challenge from Fred to take the next English side to Australia where the game's first two official Test Matches were played. Now, with the former Victoria fast bowler Jack Conway as manager and Lillywhite as the English agent, the Australians were paying a first return visit, though without any Tests in their thirty-seven fixtures.

In late May 1878, with Agnes in Kingswood Hill expecting their third child any day, W.G. met the Australians for the first time when captaining M.C.C. at Lord's. Still nursing wounds from his own tour, when his relationship with Jack Conway had been particularly difficult, he was determined to give the upstarts a real thrashing. There were about a thousand spectators in the ground, enjoying sunshine that was to make a wet wicket extremely difficult, when the Australians, fielding first, were led out led by Dave Gregory, father of sixteen children and a striking figure with his long, red beard. His sun-scorched team had all invested money in the venture and would be betting heavily on their matches in the hopes of maximizing their profits. W.G. might envisage a satisfying thrashing, but Dave Gregory's Hole-In-The-Wall Gang meant business.

It is hard for us, at Lord's today, to imagine the ground as it was when W.G. and 'Monkey' Hornby strode confidently out to the wicket to open the innings and show the Australians how to play the game. None of the grandstands survive from that period, and reports of W.G. at Lord's in the 1870s suggest some very odd-sounding features. He had sent the ball 'under the wall past the pavilion to the sheep pen in the north-east corner'; to 'Dark's Corner and Dark's House'; to 'the wood-stacks', 'the tennis court' and 'Knatchbull's corner'; to 'the armoury' and 'the nursery palings'; to 'the bat-stacks' and 'stable'; to the 'racquet court' where, on one occasion, the ball had disappeared through an open door, enabling a large number of runs. Similarly, he had once sent a ball ricocheting through an entrance gate and down St John's Wood Road as he and his partner kept on running.

This time, however, he was not his usual imperious self. His first ball he sent happily enough to square-leg for an all-run 4, but the second, lifting viciously off a length, was fended off into short-leg's eager hands. Wickets continued to tumble and M.C.C. were bowled out for 33. The public were aghast, the members tight-lipped. The news spread and the crowd quickly quadrupled. When the Australians, in their turn, came and went for 41, the public relaxed and the members resumed their chatter. But worse mayhem was in store. W.G. was bowled by Spofforth for 0; M.C.C. collapsed humiliatingly, to be all out 19; and the Australians soon knocked off the 12 they needed.

W.G. immediately asked for a rematch, but this was declined, allowing him to return to Kingswood, from where he had been cabled that he had a daughter. Still reeling from the humiliation at Lord's, he struggled to take in the good news of Bessie's arrival. In a single day a mere eleven Australians, not fifteen or eighteen but a mere eleven, had somehow routed England's premier club. Spofforth had taken 10 wickets for 20 runs. It was an unthinkable disaster.

Two weeks later W.G. met Gregory's men again, this time at Prince's, captaining a Gentlemen of England eleven that included E.M., The Colonel and Frizzy Bush. The Prince brothers had developed an aristocratic club in Knightsbridge, on a field at the back of Harrod's with an entrance in Hans Place. The pitch was 'topped with the very best Down turf available in the country'. It was home for the Household Brigade and, for a few seasons, Middlesex, and offered much more than cricket with its shady, tree-lined walks, racquets courts and a rink for the current craze of roller-skating. It was an ideal resting-place after a ride in Hyde Park. 'Under the elms of Prince's' was synonymous with high society romance, until the ground was swallowed up in housing development.

Eleven thousand spectators braved the showers on the first day. 'Many of them,' it was noted, 'were of the highest quality.' In the sodden conditions the demon Spofforth proved less effective than W.G.'s wily slow-medium and the big-spinning off-breaks and leg-breaks of Allan Steel, last season's captain of Marlborough College. W.G. top-scored with 25 and the Gentlemen of England won a low-scoring match comfortably. Some English honour had been salvaged, but bad feelings persisted.

During the match W.G. had ruminated discontentedly on the presence in the Australian side of Billy Midwinter, a giant all-rounder. Having dual qualifications, Midwinter had been a Gloucestershire professional in 1877 and, although now one of the tourists' twelve, he was selected, most confrontationally, by W.G. for the county's next match, with Surrey at The Oval, when the Australians naturally expected him to play against Middlesex at Lord's. On the morning of the matches, the Australian manager took a cab to The Oval to inform W.G. that Midwinter would stay at Lord's. The outraged W.G. told Conway that the Australians were 'a lot of sneaks'. 'High words' were said to have ensued on both sides. Events then became farcical. Conway's cab, returning to Lord's, was followed by another, bearing W.G., E.M. and Frizzy Bush. Midwinter, padded up and ready to bat, was harangued in the Lord's dressing-room for fifteen minutes. 'That Grace lost his temper and sadly forgot himself,' wrote an eye-witness, 'there can be no doubt. Nothing could justify Grace's passion and language.' But he got his way. Shortly afterwards, still padded and with cricket-bag in hand, Midwinter accompanied his three new team-mates to a waiting cab. As they reached The Oval another cab overtook them, bearing Conway, Gregory and Boyle. 'High words' ensued again, but eventually the three kidnappers and the bemused and now pad-less Midwinter ran out at The Oval to join the rest of the Gloucestershire team. The Hole-in-the-Wall Gang were down to eleven for the rest of their tour. They would settle scores when they visited Bristol.

* * *

The Grace family was out in earnest among crowds of 5,000 when, in early September, Dave Gregory's men came to Clifton for the grudge match. Jim Lillywhite was so anxious to minimise the terrible antagonisms that he decided to act as one of the umpires. 'The two stands were thronged with a fashionable assemblage,' wrote the *Bristol Mercury*, 'including very many ladies, and the circle round the ground was very densely packed.' The match, however, was to prove a disappointment to the locals. W.G. had just gashed his leg in an accident with a horse and was not at his best, suffering the irritation of an lbw decision from Jim Lillywhite and the humiliation of losing his middle stump to Spofforth. E.M. batted defiantly – 'Why don't you play like that always, Teddy,' enquired W.G., 'instead of trying to slog everything for six?' – but the Australians won in only two days. It was Gloucestershire's first defeat at Clifton and tensions were high at the formal post-match dinner. Whilst one bearded captain caroused jubilantly, the other brooded dark thoughts. 'W.G. didn't come off this time,' cried Dave Gregory during the speeches to the merriment of his gang, 'but the game has been played in a manly spirit!' To a crescendo of guffaws from one corner of the marquee, W.G. rose with as much dignity as he could muster. 'I hope ere many years,' he replied, eyeing his opposite number severely, 'another Australian team will come and be beaten.'

* * *

At the end of 1878 there were further rumours of impending retirement. W.G.'s weight was said to have risen to nearly fourteen and a half stone, and *Lillywhite's Annual*, in revealing the likelihood that he would limit himself to county matches in 1879, suggested that his best years were now over. Indeed, his total demise was probably at hand:

> The charm of Mr W.G. Grace's marvellous success with the bat seems at last to have been broken and it is open to doubt if he will regain the form of 1876 and 1877. Phenomenon as he has been, he cannot last for ever, and increasing weight with corresponding loss of elasticity must have a sensible effect upon his powers of batting . . . Whether or not he retires next year from all but county cricket, whether he be as successful or less successful than of old, the public will remember him as not only for twelve years the best all-round player of his day, but the most wonderful cricketer that ever lived.

The forecast for 1879 was not far wrong. W.G. played no games for M.C.C. or the United South, but in addition to his ten county matches (in which he still managed an average of just under 50), he also turned out in a handful of games for various sides of Gentlemen. *Lillywhite's Companion* declared him 'still the best bat in England', but added darkly that he was 'not so certain as a few years back – perhaps a little shaky now at first and tires sooner.'

For W.G. 1879 passed in a flurry of excitements: outrage in January, when he and Teddy had to beat off a serious revolt from the Gloucestershire committee who complained, of all things, of their high-handedness; fury in April, when the new editor of *Lillywhite's Companion* – a young upstart who had been in the Australians' pocket all summer and shared their distress at the kidnapping of Midwinter – made a vicious attack on his bogus amateur status; disappointment that May at the necessary handover of the United South to Fred and The Colonel; relief in July, when up in Edinburgh he wrote some satisfactory papers and held his own in a perilous viva to become a Licentiate of the Royal College of Physicians; delight the same month at the presentation during his National Testimonial match at Lord's (Over 30s v. Under 30s) of a cheque for no less than £1,700; relief on the second day of the same match when an early morning viva with the Royal College of Surgeons passed off smoothly; and exultation late summer with the addition of the letters MRCS to the already acquired LRCP. He was a doctor at last.

A doctor at last, and still a cricketer, too. The prolonged rumours of impending retirement, which had so startled and stunned the public and helped at the same time to raise the National Testimonial Fund to its high figure, were soon a thing of the past. The whole nation rejoiced that the new decade of the 1880s would not, after all, see Dr. W.G. Grace laying aside his bat and pads.

9

A Doctor at Last

Difficult years at Stapleton Road, 1879-84

In the strongly multicultural district of Easton, not far from where the M32 meets the centre of Bristol, the 'Living Easton Timesigns', a trail of illustrated plaques, help stimulate interest in the district's past. One of them, erected on Stapleton Road at the front of the Easton Leisure Centre car-park, marks the site of W.G.'s home and medical practice (knocked down in the 1970s). The plaque shows a smartly dressed W.G. with his doctor's Gladstone bag in the foreground, off to pay his patients a visit. Behind him there is a street scene of the 1880s, revealing us the way W.G.'s Stapleton Road might have looked, and there is Agnes, too, coming up to him, perhaps, with some urgent, last-minute message. The portraits in bas relief are a good reminder that they were still a young couple when they first came to Stapleton Road in the autumn of 1879, Agnes just twenty-five and W.G. thirty-one. The splendid plaque, the work of local sculptor Bryan Rawlings, was unveiled in 2000 by Tony Brown, a former Gloucestershire captain and the County Chairman at that time.

Bryan Rawlings recalls that the difficult commission stipulated that the central image should be of W.G. with his wife and a street scene, all enclosed in a cricket ball.

I had a number of images of W.G. to refer to, but only one picture of both his wife and old Easton. I reversed the latter as a mirror image so that Mrs Grace would be looking at W.G. and, at the same time, not blocking the side of the street with all the interesting shapes of shop blinds. I formed the 'ball' border in plaster, the central details being modelled in plasticene on this plaster base, and the finished article came from a GRP (fibreglass) mould.

Bryan's plaque is not easy to find, for Stapleton Road has been cut in two by the dual carriageway of the A4320. The Lawrence Hill Roundabout makes a useful starting-point. From there we follow Easton Way (the A4320) in the direction of the M32, but, before we reach the motorway, take a left-hand turning for 'West Stapleton Road'. The Leisure Centre is just a few hundred yards on our left.

Its car park is, in fact, built over two different houses, 61 and 57 Stapleton Road, in which the Graces lived (first at 61, but mostly at 57), situated within the same small terrace on the east side of the road, just above the junction with Thrissell Street. The houses had no front garden and only a modest one to the rear, with access to a back passageway leading into Thrissell Street. Space was at a premium in 61. Aunt Caroline and Uncle John had made the move from Acton to Bristol with the family of five; Agnes' younger brother Stewart was staying with them as a medical apprentice; and there were three domestic servants to accommodate, as well as W.G.'s ground floor surgery. Two years later, therefore, in late 1881, they moved two houses up the terrace, to Thrissell House, 57 Stapleton Road, which was much more capacious.

There, in the months outside the cricket season, W.G. worked hard as a Public Vaccinator and the Medical Officer for the Barton Regis Union. In true Pocock spirit, he and Agnes had opted for one of the city's less prosperous areas, a working-class district about two miles from Downend, dominated by railways and coal-mines. Down Thrissell Street and along Easton Road were the Bristol Wagon Works. A few hundred yards to the south were the goods sheds of St Philip's Station. Just up Stapleton Road were the Pennywell and Easton collieries, an integral part of W.G.'s practice. The Graces had blacksmiths, railway clerks, butchers and shoemakers among their neighbours. It was a busy and lively community, short of money but happy to have emerged from the slums into modern accommodation, however crowded. 'From early morn till late in the evening, you will find W.G. toiling at his profession,' wrote Brownlee, 'trudging through rain, sunshine and storm, as cheerful and buoyant as if he were playing cricket . . . No brighter or more unselfish spirit lives on the face of this earth of ours.' The people of Easton would have agreed. Their exuberant doctor, for all his celebrity, related easily to them and, for all his financial acumen, would waive payment from those in direst difficulties.

* * *

W.G.'s early seasons in the new decade, though not as outstandingly productive as usual, included, in September 1880, the first Test Match ever played in this country, when sixty thousand spectators attended The Oval over the three days, to see England, captained by Lord Harris, take on the Australians. We can be confident that Martha and Uncle Alfred were among those watching intently, for, although both were now well into their sixties, they would not have missed one ball of such an important match in which three Graces were playing. Seen through their eyes, the historic Test was a never-to-be-forgotten occasion.

Pride was uppermost initially. There they were, Gilbert and Teddy, opening for England and batting with their usual nonchalance. It was like old times on Durdham Down, except that Teddy, with his uncle's latest advice ringing in his ears, was somehow managing to keep the ball on the ground. There *was* one moment of anxiety, when E.M. rashly called for a single that wasn't there and nearly ran out W.G. 'I quite agree he should tell Teddy off, Alfred, but he does seem to be doing so rather lengthily.' And then more undiluted pleasure, with some lovely drives from Gilbert. 'I am a little anxious, Martha, for Gilbert is outpacing Teddy, and Teddy won't like that at all. He could become rash.' And, alas, he did. There were the usual deep sighs from Uncle Alfred as E.M. holed out impetuously for 36, though Martha rejoiced at the 91 the two of them had put on together in 90 minutes. 'There was no *need* for that, Martha. His foot was nowhere near the pitch of the ball.' 'Don't tell *me*, Alfred, tell *him*!' Joy soon returned, however, for Gilbert was in beautiful touch. His square cuts positively sizzled. 'And that's a delightful late cut, Martha.' 'Delicate, indeed, Alfred. His bat could have been a wisp of hay as he caressed the ball to the ring.' 'As delicate as one of father's biggest kites, dear, swooping down in a gentle breeze on a May morning.' When things were going particularly well, their poetic inclinations found ready expression, and by the luncheon interval, when Gilbert was on 81, brother and sister were in full flight. The light grew poor in the afternoon, but there was more delight as W.G. moved confidently on to 152. Four o'clock had passed before disaster struck 'He's lost his off stump, Alfred! He's lost his off stump! Oh dear, where are my smelling salts?' 'My dear Martha, don't distress yourself. It looked a *good* ball. No dishonour in getting out to a *good* ball.' 'You're quite right, Alfred, and in this terrible light, too, he really did bat most extremely well.' 'Quite so, quite so. We must rejoice to have seen such a copybook innings. Technically perfect. And now that England are so well placed, perhaps we might stroll over and have a word with the dear boys?'

The first day ended in darkness and drizzle. Fred had the bad luck to come in just before the close, with England 410-8 and night setting in. 'It's outrageous, Alfred, for them to be batting poor Fred so low. Outrageous!' 'I agree, dear, absolutely. But don't distress yourself.' 'You must speak to Lord Harris, Alfred. You must tell him it isn't right.' 'I'll try to catch him, dear, in the morning.' 'Fetch me the chocolate candies, Alfred. They're in a box in my bag.' 'Whereabouts in your bag, dear? Are you quite sure you didn't polish them off mid-afternoon?' 'Oh no! No chocolate candies, Alfred! My smelling salts instead!' 'A problem, Martha?' 'I'm afraid that while your head was in my bag, searching for candies that I certainly can't remember polishing off in the afternoon, poor Freddy has been caught at slip. First ball.' 'First ball? At slip?' 'At slip. First ball. And now they're coming off! All thanks to that idiot Lord Harris!'

They were there, of course, for the second day, when in reply to England's 420, Australia were bowled out for 149, the turning-point coming halfway through the innings when, to Martha and Alfred's overwhelming delight, the great hitter Bonnor lofted Alfred Shaw high in the direction of the gasometers, and Fred, sprinting flat out along the boundary, brought off the catch of the season. Australia followed on, and when Martha and Alfred returned for the last day, a triumphant early finish seemed likely, with Australia still nearly 100 behind and with only 4 wickets left. An exasperating morning, however, saw Gilbert coming in for some heavy punishment from Billy Murdoch and the beginning of a last-wicket stand that eventually put on 88, keeping England in the field till 3.00 p.m. England now needed 57 to win. It was not much of an ask, and Martha and Alfred settled down to enjoy the rest of the afternoon.

There was one small problem. 'I seem to have left my lorgnette in the pavilion, Alfred.' 'I'll get it for you, my dear, at the end of the first over.' 'But who's this coming out, Alfred? What's happening? Where are Gilbert and Teddy?' 'You told me to speak to Harris, Martha, so of course I did. I told him we jolly well felt that poor Fred had had a rough deal.' 'And so?' 'And so, my dear, Martha, that's Freddy you see out there – or, rather, don't see – opening with the Honourable Alfred Lyttelton. Harris has taken the point and changed the batting order!' 'But I didn't want Gilbert *not* to open, Alfred!' 'Shush, Martha! I thought it would make a pleasant surprise. Harris is holding Teddy and Gilbert in reserve. It's a piece of cake, of course, with only 57 needed, and Harris decided, very generously, that Fred could lead us to victory. And they seem to be making . . . they seemed to have been making . . . ' He tailed off miserably. 'What's up, Alfred? Have we lost a wicket? It rather looks as if we may have done so.' 'Oh, heavens, yes, we have indeed. How very unfortunate. With so few runs on the board, too.' 'Is it that Lyttelton fellow, Alfred? I've always thought he was too glamorous by half to be reliable.' 'Well no, my dear. I don't want to spoil your afternoon like this, but I'm afraid there's no way of altering the unpalatable fact that the unfortunate Fred has been the one to go.' '*Fred*, Alfred?' 'Yes, dear.' 'The one to go?' 'Yes, dear, I'm afraid so. It's what comes from playing down the wrong line. There are two runs on the board, so that's a start, but I'm afraid to say not one of them is actually Fred's. The poor lad has got a pair . . .'

Further disasters made Martha rather wish that Alfred hadn't recovered her lorgnette. It was too awful. Among a flurry of wickets, out had stridden a belligerent E.M. only to be forgetful of his uncle's very latest advice and soon to be striding back again, bowled for 0. With England 31-5 Gilbert had at last emerged, but Martha was too upset at the ignominy of England's champion coming in at seven to enjoy watching him and his partner, Kent amateur Frank Penn, bringing England swiftly towards victory. 'It's outrageous, Alfred, Gilbert batting so low, and, of course, it's all your fault. If only you hadn't got Harris to muddle things up, Fred would never have got a pair and Gilbert would have been opening the batting with Teddy, keeping him in order.' 'Please don't upset yourself, my dear. That was a fine cut by Gilbert. Only one to win now.' 'Find me my handkerchief from my bag, Alfred. The black lace one.' 'Yes, dear. Of course. The boys mustn't see you've been getting upset. It would quite spoil their day.' 'The winning hit, Alfred, and your head was in the bag!' 'Would a purple one do, dear? I can't find the black one.' 'Oh my! What's this great kerfuffle, Alfred?' 'It's only the crowd expressing their relief, dear, that Gilbert has triumphed and England are victorious. Why, I do believe they're going to hoist him onto their shoulders. How wonderful!' 'Wonderful, Alfred? Hoisting Gilbert onto their shoulders can hardly be wonderful. Are they strong enough? Can they support the dear boy's weight? Oh my! Won't they drop him and do him some dreadful injury?' 'More likely to do *themselves* an injury, I should think, Martha. Here's the black hanky!' But Martha's mood had lightened. 'Oh my! Hoisted triumphant! Carried back to the pavilion, the saviour of the nation! Find me the chocolate candies, Alfred.'

* * *

We are well to the south-west of The Oval, at Basingstoke, lunching at the 3-star Red Lion. It's a pub that is under new management and flourishing once more after some difficult times. It is a splendid former coaching inn in the heart of the town, and much of it is little changed from when, shortly after the Oval Test in 1880, Fred stayed there.

He had travelled back to Gloucestershire directly after the Test for United South's three-day fixture against a twenty-two of Stroud. He was not feeling well – he had not been feeling good at The Oval – but struggled on with a heavy cold, taking a number of Stroud wickets and top-scoring with 44. After two days' convalescence back at The Chesnuts, he had headed off against Martha's advice for a benefit match at Winchester, stopping overnight at the Red Lion so that he could catch up with some Basingstoke friends, against whom, a few weeks before, he had been playing for the United South. Unfortunately the journey went badly, with a long wait on Reading Station in the cold and rain. When one of the young Basingstoke cricketers, Dr Charles Webb, called in to see him at the Red Lion, he was shocked at how ill Fred seemed and persuaded him to stay in bed the next day and forget about the Winchester match.

Two days later Fred had not improved, and Dr Webb, on discovering that one lung was affected by what he now feared was pneumonia, made urgent contact with the family. Wally Gilbert, who was living at The Chesnuts, rushed down to the Red Lion at once. Henry visited the following day, but W.G. decided to turn out for Bedminster in a Bristol club match. He took little pleasure, however, in his many runs and wickets. His young brother was clearly far from well. It was fortunate, of course, that he was as strong as an ox, and it was reassuring that Henry would be there again, bringing his experience to the situation. It was good, too, that the admirable Wally had promised to stay down at the hotel until Fred could come home.

The next morning there was an encouraging telegram from Wally. A day later, another visit from Henry found Fred 'worse', but 'no immediate danger was apprehended'. Some encouragement followed. After a week at the Red Lion, The Colonel reported happily that Fred had 'spent a good night, and was much better'. But the next night, as he and landlord Sam Andrews stood by helplessly, the pneumonia, now in both lungs, accelerated. Alerted to the crisis in the early morning, W.G. set out at once for Bradford-on-Avon, where Henry was staying, intending to go across to Basingstoke with him. But just after lunch on 22 September, in the presence of Wally Gilbert, landlord Sam Andrews and Dr Charles Webb, Fred died. W.G. and Henry were on the platform of Bradford-upon-Avon station when they heard the news.

* * *

Christ Church Vicarage, built for the Danns and their several young daughters only the previous year, lies about a hundred yards away along Downend Road from the entrance to the churchyard, in the opposite direction from The Chesnuts. A generously-proportioned vicarage, it became surplus to requirements and today serves as a day nursery school. Here at the old vicarage, in one of its quieter moments, it is easy to imagine John Dann gently comforting Blanche, as they made their way, as so often before, to The Chesnuts, only this time with the distressing prospect of helping lead the mournful procession escorting Fred's coffin across the road to Christ Church.

The village was overflowing with Fred's relatives and cricketing friends, and Downend Road was full of hushed mourners as the procession began. There was just one carriage behind the coffin, carrying the distraught Martha and Fred's fiancée, Annie Robinson. Swathed in black (just as she would later be swathed in white when becoming E.M.'s second bride), Annie Robinson was the eldest daughter of a rich Bristol paper manufacturer, whose family was so devoted to cricket they sometimes ran a whole team of Robinsons. Annie herself was an avid cricket enthusiast as well as an energetic rider to hounds. The winding pathway that led inside the churchyard was also lined with silent well-wishers, and many of the three thousand who had gathered to honour Fred had to wait outside Christ Church during the service, for every pew was tightly packed, both downstairs and in the three-sided gallery.

John Dann was an engaging speaker but he struggled in the service to apply a Christian sense of consolation to the death of the twenty-nine-year-old who had just played for England, breaking down completely at one stage. For W.G. himself, grief was compounded by his failure to visit Fred during his short final illness. We can imagine his distressed thoughts as he followed the coffin out of the church and towards Dr Henry's grave. Fred had just taken some medical exams that year, and seemed likely to follow him very shortly in settling down as a doctor. He had so much to live for. So much vitality to give the world. It would be hard to imagine a future without him. There would be no Fred next week, for example, at the partridge shooting over the Duke of Beaufort's Dormalin property, courtesy of the Duke himself, a day's pleasure each September that they so often had shared together with Teddy and Alfred. And no Fred next cricket season. Unthinkable. The two had been inseparable for so many years. He remembered watching on with pride as Fred played in the Canterbury week before he was sixteen and then again for the county before he was seventeen. It had always been extra fun when Fred was in the team! And even more so on the rare occasions they opposed each other! This had happened at Bedminster only three months ago when Fred and The Colonel had brought the United South there, and Teddy and he had opened the innings for the Bedminster Eighteen. He had twice caught and bowled Fred. So much fun. So many games. So much to remember . . . It was almost a relief when John Dann completed the graveside ritual, and they made their way, with difficulty, through the dark, teeming crowd and down the road to The Chesnuts . . .

* * *

Martha never fully recovered from the tragedy. She would commune every day at the grave of her son and husband, and when she herself died four years later, aged seventy-two, she was buried in the same resting-place. The grave, today, is tightly hemmed in by others and goes unnoticed. It would seem to have had attention at some time in the past, for the tribute to George Frederick Grace is strongly legible. It is less easy to read his parents' inscriptions.

W.G. had been batting with Wally Gilbert at Old Trafford in the middle of the afternoon on the second day of a county match there, when there came an unexpected stoppage, the Lancashire captain, Hornby, suddenly leaving the field. E.M., who had just been caught and was back in the pavilion had received a telegram with the news of Martha's death. Hornby dashed back to tell the two batsmen. After a brief consultation it was agreed that the match should be abandoned. It was a touching gesture, but one that Martha herself would have fiercely criticised. If her dear son and nephew had played on, they could have put the county in a winning position by the close of play.

Martha's death had taken the family of doctors by surprise. Though she had been in poor health for some time, she had still been able to follow her sons' cricket with her usual care and pride. Gilbert's form since Fred's death had been a little disappointing, but then he had so many preoccupations, what with his hard work over the winter months, his negotiations with the county over the funding of his summer locums, and the arrival of their third son, the adorable little Charles, who had been born in Stapleton Road two years ago, soon after they left 61 for Thrissell House.

She had approved of the move. It was always important for a family to have space at its disposal for its emergencies, and their new fourteen-year lease gave them security. The house was a merger of two separate buildings and there was the strong possibility in the fullness of time of the use of the adjacent Thrissell Lodge (number 55), which would do perfectly for Gilbert's practice. Meanwhile they had taken her advice and turned the back lawn of Thrissell House into a cricket net, good enough for the county players to come and use. Agnes had sensibly put her foot down – she was good at doing that – and decreed that no players should come through the house – they could use the Thrissell Street back entrance. She had also expressed concern when balls started coming through the kitchen windows. These were soon protected by railings.

Gilbert's loss of his best form over the years since poor Fred's death was as disappointing to Martha as it was understandable. Just a small, temporary loss, of course. In 1881 he was still second in the 1st-class averages. *Lillywhite's Annual* loyally had declared there had been 'no marked decline noticeable in his batting', though Martha was less pleased at the *Lillywhite's Companion*'s allusions to his sixteen-stone frame: 'Time is apt to build a bow-window in the temple of the body; and a certain *embonpoint* which is stealing over the Gloucestershire eleven illustrates the general application of the truth.' That was something better left out of the latest album! It was ungainsayable, however, that the next season

Downend House, the Graces' home 1831–50.

Clematis House (the white house behind the far batsman) overlooking the W.G. Grace Memorial Ground, Downend.

The Willows Shopping Centre, Downend, with the Grace ceramic mural featuring The Chesnuts (which was sited just behind the telephone building, far left).

The Wellingbrough School cricket pavilion with the engraved doorstep of The Chesnuts (inset) at the very bottom of the steps.

The site of the United South's game at Northampton with the original racecourse pavilion (inset).

The *Great Britain* on which E.M. sailed to Australia. W.G.'s visits there were undertaken on ships of similar size.

The first-class dining room of the *Great Britain*, the wax model suggesting something of Agnes Grace in 1873.

Above left: A recent photograph of the Dutch elm planted by Grace at the Eastern Oval, Ballarat, Australia in 1874 (photo: Keith Rees).

Above right: A statue of W.G. Grace's godfather, William Gilbert Rees, at Queenstown, New Zealand (photo: Rosemary Marryatt).

E.M. Grace's ground at Thornbury, Alveston, with the adjacent Ship Inn (inset).

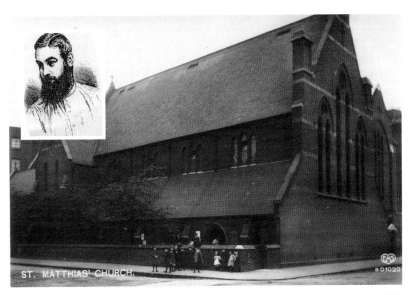

St Matthias' Church, West Brompton, where W.G. Grace married Agnes Day in 1873. Inset: W.G. at the time of his wedding.

The Graces' home in Acton.

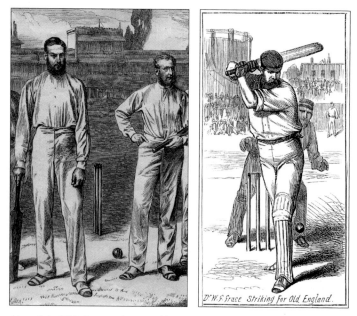

Above left: W.G. Grace and V.E. 'Teddy' Walker at Lord's in 1871.

Above right: A less than totally successful representation of Grace batting at the first ever Test Match in England, at The Oval, September 1880. (*Penny Illustrated Paper*).

Right: 'In memoriam. G.F. Grace. Bowled!' A tribute to W.G.'s brother in the *Penny Illustrated Paper*, 2 October 1880.

Below: A detail from Bryan Rawlings' plaque, Stapleton Road, Bristol.

Stapleton Road and Thrissell Street, Bristol. W.G.'s surgery (at No. 55 Stapleton Road) was at the corner of the two roads.

The memorial in front of the Easton Leisure Centre marking the site of No. 57, Stapleton Road, where the Graces lived 1881–94.

Above: Part of a 1999 mural by Bill Guilding at Stapleton Road station, Bristol, celebrating the community. Grace helped out at the Easton Colliery explosion of 1886, mentioned on the left.

Right: The grave of G.F. Grace and his parents, Christ Church, Downend.

Sheffield Park, Sussex, May 1893: Lord Sheffield's Eleven versus the Australians. Inset: the roller recently restored to the ground.

John Walter Dann, Vicar of Christ Church and creator of Downend's cricket ground. (Photo: Bob Pigeon)

Above left: The Graces' home in Victoria Square, Clifton. On the extreme right: the arch that leads to the Clifton Arcade.

Above right: Roger Gibbons, Hon. Archivist of Gloucestershire C.C.C., with W.G. Grace's famous bat of 1895.

Kingswood Hill, Bristol: in the centre of the seat on the left behind the bus shelter, a stone from Henry Grace's old home reads 'Mr Grace's surgery'.

The entrance to Ashley House, near the county ground, Bristol. The houses on the extreme left mark the site of the Graces' home, Ashley Grange (inset).

Above left: An illustration from 1899 shows the public interest in Grace's new venture. (*Penny Illustrated Paper*)

Above right: Fairmount at the time of the unveiling of the plaque, summer 1966. Left to right: G. Neville Weston, the Revd Neville Sugden, Stuart Chiesman (photo: John Kennett)

The National Sports Centre, Crystal Palace, looks down on the site of Grace's pavilion (behind the two cricket players)

Crystal Palace: the opposite view, looking towards the site of the pavilion and the cricket ground beyond.

W.G. Grace in beautifully balanced action, playing against the West Indians at the Crystal Palace 1900. Alas, only empty benches witness his artistry.

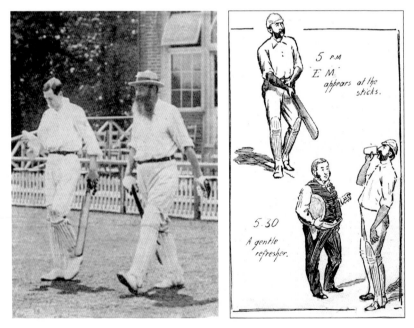

Above left: [Another equally rare photograph] W.G. Grace and his opening partner, Major James Gilman, at the same match.

Above right: E.M. Grace, 'the coroner' and 'little doctor'.

Roger Gibbons at the Bristol County Ground with the ball that received harsh treatment during W.G. Grace's hundredth 100.

Fairmount, Mottingham, W.G. Grace's last home.

Above left: Christ Church's sexton Steve Powell sadly surveys E.M. Grace's gravestone which, by Health and Safety decree, has been taken down from an upright position.

Above right: The Grace grave at Elmers End, Beckenham, a brilliant white among much grey.

The Grace grave shines in the distance. The procession with the coffin had come up the curving path, lined with mourners, from the cemetery chapel (just behind the trees) and turned abruptly right to the grave through another avenue of mourners.

his average slumped to 26 and for the first time for fifteen years, he had failed to score a century, but the *Companion* was surely going too far in suggesting 'he was beginning to feel the advance of years', was becoming defensive and had seemingly 'lost his marvellous power of scoring off good balls'. How could he have so deteriorated when, as the editor admitted, he was 'still the best batsmen in England'? It was a pity, of course, that Gilbert hadn't steered England to victory at The Oval in that match against Australia, when they failed by 7 runs to make the 85 they needed. But Gilbert had top-scored with 31. If only he'd not played that rash stroke to mid-off, if only he'd directed the drive past Bannerman, all that nonsense in the *Sporting Times* about the death of English cricket and 'the body being cremated' and the 'ashes taken to Australia' would never have happened.

It was true that last year some younger rivals were threatening to usurp his supreme position, that the bowling had fallen away a little, and the runs were flowing less readily. But, as the *Annual* so rightly stated in its latest edition, 'in batting he still has no superiors'.

* * *

That winter there had been one particularly joyful occasion at Christ Church for Martha, when John Dann had officiated at the marriage of Wally Gilbert and Sarah Lillywhite. Since the death of her sister Rose, Martha had happily acted as Wally's mother. He was, of course, something of a scatter-brained rogue, but she had always been fond of him, admired his all-round cricketing abilities and was delighted that he continued to live at The Chesnuts with her and her daughter Fanny. His gaiety was some compensation for the loss of Fred. It was marvellous that this marriage was uniting two famous cricketing families, even if the Lillywhites were very much on the professional side of the fence. Sarah was the daughter of Jem Lillywhite who had made such a big success of his coaching at Cheltenham College, his flourishing sports outfitters in the town and in the creation of the Cheltenham Festival. His death in harness, only the year before, had been widely deplored.

Martha had high hopes for what the marriage might do for her poor Walter. He had been deeply shaken by Fred's tragic death. On and off the field they had been more twins than cousins. The Colonel was just as extrovert a character as Fred had been, the only one of the four Graces who, in the early Cheltenham Festivals, had had the courage to appear on the stage of the Theatre Royal, playing leading roles in farces specially put on for the cricketing fraternity. Walter had proved himself a real stage star! But Fred's death had changed everything. Now he was drowning his sorrow in spirits, though he no longer had the money to pay for it all. He was also mixing with no-goods like Jupp and Pooley. The United South had died with Fred, so Walter had lost out there. He'd been working as a salesman without much success. He'd also started his own travelling team, the United Eleven of All-England, but, despite some occasional help from Gilbert and Teddy, that too had been an expensive flop. Maybe the marriage would save him. Maybe he could still hold together his precarious Gloucestershire career? She would have to speak to Gilbert about him. Surely he could help save Walter from his demons?

In her final months Martha had been able to take pleasure from W.G.'s promising start to the new season of 1884. The centuries were flowing again. 111 at Bedminster for the county versus Twenty-two Colts of Gloucestershire; 101 versus the Australians at Lord's for M.C.C.; a further 107 against them for the Gentlemen of England at The Oval. And 136 playing for Teddy's Thornbury against Chepstow, making a big stand with poor Walter, who also scored a century.

* * *

Gilbert, Teddy and Wally absented themselves from the next two county matches after Martha's death. When he returned, W.G. soon showed it was going to be business as usual, with 117 in a warm-up game for East Somerset against Wells and an undefeated 116 the next day against the Australians at Clifton, which made up for his lack of a big score against them in the Test Matches. His final matches of the season were of the usual wide variety, moving from a packed Oval (where England regained the 'Ashes' in the final Test) to Bristol's quiet City and County Asylum, where he assisted John Dann's side in its annual fixture there. But for the first time in his career, there was no Martha to pore over the latest book of cuttings, charting his every innings.

* * *

Martha's death meant the end of the Graces' tenure of The Chesnuts. Fanny moved to Downend where, at Grove Villa, close to the Vicarage, she kept boarders to help pay the rent.

We have come to Wellingborough in Northamptonshire. W.G. did once play against a twenty-two of Wellingborough in his 1876 heyday, but that was on a ground that disappeared years ago. Facing us is the attractively thatched pavilion at Wellingborough School. It had only been in use ten years when, in 1939, the school's cricket master heard that W.G.'s old home in Downend was being demolished, dashed down there and magnificently rescued the front doorstep of The Chesnuts from the bulldozers and had the narrow grey stone, suitably inscribed, installed at the bottom of the pavillion's steps. Over the past seventy-five years cricketers at the school have stood on W.G.'s old doorstep in the hope that it would bring them luck. It is only a little memento, yet a unique and wonderful tribute, its carefully carved inscription reminding us that W.G. was 'not of an age but for all time'. It brings us very close to Dr Henry, Martha and their remarkable family.

10

A Blight on the Glory

New triumphs and old weaknesses, 1885–89

Martha's optimism during the relatively disappointing early Stapleton Road years proved justified. In 1885, the year after her death, the thirty-seven-year-old W.G. enjoyed what the *Memorial Biography* was to call 'a second zenith', his average of 43 for his 1,700 runs putting him third in the country, his 117 wickets bringing him another double. His undefeated 221 against Middlesex at Clifton, when he opened the innings with The Colonel and was still at the crease undefeated when the last wicket eventually fell the next day, was just one of twenty-one hundreds he was to score in his great renaissance of 1885–89.

* * *

The Grand in Bristol's Broad Street is a flourishing hotel, part of the Thistle Group, with 180 bedrooms and an impressive list of former guests that includes Sir Winston Churchill and The Beatles. Back in 1873 the recently-built hotel, then known as the White Lion, was the very latest thing in luxury. The manager could address his staff via a new-fangled 'speaking tube'; there was quite the finest wine cellar in Bristol and the hotel's popular new cocktails included The Cliftonian – a delicious mix of Grand Marnier, punch and orange juice. That it was the venue selected by the three Graces for Gloucestershire's annual meetings and dinners (a tradition that was to last sixty years) says much about their ambitions for the county. The hotel was the scene of many spirited battles of will. On one famous occasion the entire committee responded to E.M.'s high-handedness by boycotting a meeting. 'Present: E.M. Grace, and that's all,' he later wrote cheerfully in the Minute Book.

It was at the Grand, in the summer of 1885, that the final act in the tragedy of Wally Gilbert had its beginning. The Graces had put before the committee a proposal that their beleaguered cousin should be given enhanced expenses for the new season. The Committee turned the proposal down. The desperate Wally thereupon suggested to his cousins that he might have to surrender his amateur status and turn professional. The social ramifications of the move were immense. He would be joining the working classes. W.G. was appalled. But if this was a last-ditch attempt to elicit some financial support from the family, it failed, for in January 1886 The Colonel's new status was announced. He would play for Gloucestershire as a professional. He would also be employed in a similar capacity by East Gloucestershire, an exclusive club whose members came from Cheltenham society.

In early June 1886 The Colonel turned up at East Gloucestershire's Charlton Park ground, just down the road from Cheltenham College.* Only the week before he had top-scored and taken six wickets for the club against an Oxford college side which had, however, scored a huge total and swept East Gloucestershire humiliatingly aside. The Colonel's happy-go-lucky attitude towards this setback, allied to his heavy drinking, may well have upset several members, including the club secretary, a retired army officer, Captain Harry Willes, and a young subaltern currently serving with the Bombay Staff Corps, Lieutenant William Barrington Piers. Money had been going missing for some time from the club's changing room. The disreputable new professional was the clear suspect. Willes and Piers, men of action, trained to do everything by the book, laid a trap with marked coins on the morning of the match with Stroud.

A police sergeant, hiding in the changing-room loft, duly spotted Wally readying himself for the match, waiting till he was alone and then going through various waistcoats and trousers. Confronted by the two club members and their policeman, he confessed at once, handing back two sovereigns and a shilling. He admitted, likewise, to having stolen money earlier in the season and begged for leniency. He would, he said, follow the route of all criminals and go abroad, if that was what they wanted. But for the sake of his wife, a Lillywhite, and his family, the Graces . . . His characteristic cheerful swagger evaporated. He broke down, again abjectly asking for mercy, but there was to be none. The East Gloucester team went out to play Stroud with only ten men that afternoon, for The Colonel was taken into custody, pending an appearance before the magistrates on the Monday.

It is thought that W.G. may have rushed across to Cheltenham that Saturday as his match at Lord's against the Australians had finished conveniently early. But whatever behind-the-scenes involvement there may have been, when his cousin appeared on the Monday before three Cheltenham magistrates, W.G. was far away on the south coast, captaining Gloucestershire as usual. The team, however, was not just short of Wally Gilbert. At least five other regulars were missing, including E.M. None appeared in court to speak on The Colonel's behalf, but at least they felt they should not be down at Hove, distancing themselves from their troubled friend. W.G. clearly had problems in raising a side for the Hove game, having to include his twenty-year-old nephew Alfie,** his brother Alfred's son, who

---

* The cricket ground today is covered by the courts of the flourishing East Gloucestershire Tennis Club.

** A talented all-rounder in club cricket, Dr Alfie Grace (who followed his father into practice at Chipping Sodbury) was to play one further first-class match. Like his father he rode to hounds with distinction.

would score centuries for Chipping Sodbury and Thornbury but was hardly an obvious county selection.

Things went badly that Monday. Wally Gilbert made a poor impression, his heavy black beard, recently grown because of a skin complaint, only adding to a generally seedy demeanour. A hastily-found lawyer stressed in his defence his 'good family and antecedents' without actually mentioning the Graces by name. The prisoner, he declared, had for some time past been a worried and harassed man over his affairs. In drowning his troubles with drink he had lost control of his own actions. The Colonel's own words could hardly have helped his cause: 'I had not been very well on the day in question and became possessed of an irresistible impulse to take the money. It is clearly proved that I was not actuated by the motives of a common thief, or I would surely have taken more money than I did, when the opportunity was there. I would ask you to bear in mind that whatever punishment you inflict, I will be for ever estranged from my friends and acquaintances. My only option is to emigrate. . .' The Bench's chairman, George Maver Jackson, who, like the two complainants, had a background of British India, regretted he could not respond with just a fine, and so, on a day when W.G., as usual, top-scored for the county, his cousin and long-time cricketing companion went to prison to do twenty-eight days' hard labour.

Though the Graces' name was not mentioned, the local papers gave the case good coverage. *The Cheltenham Looker-On* was typical:

> Mr Gilbert's social position – though recently clouded by monetary embarrassment – and his cricketing celebrity combined with his connection by marriage with Cheltenham to render his appearance in its Police Court quite 'the talk of the town' where, as throughout the country, the announcement of his intended emigration, on the expiration of his sentence, is felt to be the only course open to him – a course which will, doubtless, be facilitated by many personal acquaintances he had made throughout Gloucestershire.

The news soon spread far beyond Gloucestershire. Everyone in the cricket world knew exactly what had happened. But W.G. remained silent on the subject, then and forever.

His own game seems not to have been affected. He made two fifties at Hove and, in the immediate aftermath, though he failed in the Old Trafford Test Match, he scored a sparkling 148, captaining The Gentlemen of England against the Australians at Lord's. At Oxford's Parks for M.C.C. he not only 'dispatched the ball time and time again to the boundary' in his 104, but bowled unchanged in the University's second innings taking all ten of their wickets. At Moreton-in-the-Marsh, a trenchant 92 not out helped avert a Gloucestershire defeat. To all appearances, The Colonel's tragedy might never have happened.

At the same time that the disgraced thirty-two-year-old was crossing the Atlantic with his wife and baby daughter to start a new life in Canada, *Cricket* magazine, touched by the national enthusiasm for Queen Victoria's imminent Golden Jubilee

and in sympathetic response to the sad events of the past few weeks, celebrated
W.G.'s thirty-eighth birthday with an emotional poem.

> W onder and pride of England's hardy race,
> I mmortal thou hast made the name of Grace.
> L o unto thee, the wide-spread nations raise
> L oud, thundering cheers of far, re-echoing praise,
> I n lands of burning sun, or frozen snow,
> A mid the winter's blast, or summer's glow,
> M yriads on thee the victor's wreath bestow.

> G reat in thy matchless and amazing skill,
> I n spite of years, without an equal still.
> L ong life and many a mighty score
> B e thine, famed batsman, on this hither shore
> E xcelling still, and gaining laurels new,
> R ecalling all and more, thy youth did do,
> T he pride of cricket, yea, its idol too!

> G o on in might! Nor with the bat alone:
> R ightly noble with the ball thou hold'st thine own,
> A nd in the field thy skill is also known
> C hampion indeed, thy fame shall truly be
> E ndless as time, far-reaching as the sea!

Untouched by his cousin's disgrace, W.G. maintained good form for the rest of
the season. Adversity always strengthened his endeavours. He ended up near the
top of the national averages for 1886, having again done the double (with 1,846
runs and 122 wickets). 'Still one of the best batsmen of the day,' commented the
Companion. 'Hits all round freely and times the ball with extraordinary precision;
bowls with great success, having a high delivery and varying his pace and pitch
with great judgment; brilliant field anywhere…'

* * *

In the Lord's Museum, currently tucked away in a corner, is a plaster of Paris
bust of W.G. dating to 1888, the year the old pavilion was being pulled down
to make way for today's iconic building. The bust is the creation of a London-
based sculptor William Tyler. Three versions are known to exist but the one we
are looking at is the Graces' own bust that was eventually presented by Agnes to
M.C.C. four years after W.G. died.

It is an informative work of art. W.G.'s heavily creased shirt, in strong contrast
to the carefully combed hair, is a quiet pointer towards the rough-and-ready

country doctor's son, not wholly a gentleman, and therefore, despite being the outstanding amateur cricket of his age, not entrusted with the captaincy of the national team until 1888, when he was forty. It also catches W.G. at the time when his public image was beginning its slow metamorphosis from the shrewdly calculating, win-at-all-costs juggernaut of a champion to the Grand Old Man with the reassuring twinkle in his eyes and the comfortable girth of an amiable Falstaff, who stood for all that was best in the benign British Empire – the Grace who was to bestride cricket's Golden Age in the 1890s and be immortalised in the *fin-de-siècle* explosion of illustrated newspapers and magazines. Here, in the Lord's Museum, we can see that transformation in progress. It is not yet complete. Despite the reassuringly immaculate hair – not a lock out of place – and the welcoming warmth of the smile, the eyes are not yet twinkling at all; indeed, they are not really looking at us; there's a shiftiness, urging us to be a little cautious. William Tyler's bust has captured W.G. at a fascinating moment when the legendary image of the G.O.M. was in the process of creation.

It is useful, too, in showing him at his 'second zenith', shortly after the very hot summer of 1887 when he had averaged 54 for his 2,062 runs and was only three wickets short of the double; when he had come second in the national averages; had scored centuries in both innings against Kent at Clifton; and had tirelessly amassed an undefeated 183 against Yorkshire at Gloucester on the hottest day of the entire sun-drenched year.

It shows us, too, the man who, in the subsequent wet summer of 1888, still managed 1,886 runs and, with cunning compensating for a lesser amount of spin, took an impressive 93 wickets (in the first season of the five-ball over). A double century that year at Hove with some eighty singles bore out *The Times*' comment that 'he exhibited quite his old self in placing the ball', while centuries in both innings against Yorkshire at Clifton (148 and 153) elicited some finely driven 4s on both sides of the wicket, including one that went high over the seats and another that halted conversation in the refreshment tent. His 154 on a worn wicket at the Scarborough Festival was as fine an innings as he had ever played. 'One doubts,' wrote *Sporting Life*, 'if, in what it now seems absurd to call his best days, he ever played better cricket.' 'Other cricketers rise, wane and disappear,' noted the magazine *Cricket*, 'but W.G. still holds the field against all comers.' He was 'almost as buoyant and full of life,' wrote *Lillywhite's Annual*, as when he was sixteen.

* * *

Since the days of Dr Henry the young county club had struggled with the thorny problem of having no home ground of its own. Well supported though the matches in August at Clifton and Cheltenham Colleges were, a ground that was available throughout the season was an urgent requirement. In 1884 W.G. had begun serving on a sub-committee tasked with finding a solution and when, four years later, the possibility arose of purchasing agricultural land on Ashley Down where the only nearby buildings were huge stone orphanages, he became a director of the specially-formed County Ground Company Committee to manage the creation of what would, in effect, become a sports centre. Ashley Down, high up to the north-west of Bristol, not very far from Durdham Down, offered a large fourteen-acre site, in which the cricketers would have exclusive use of an area 100 yards square. W.G., regularly commuting by train to Ashley Hill station, could not keep away, constantly advising, cajoling, supervising, like a king who had awarded himself a new castle and would brook no interference from his subjects in its construction. Sparks flew accordingly, but a cricket ground arose, ready for 1889, with a three-storey pavilion as its main feature (smaller than the present one, but on the same site).

For a very short while the view from the pavilion was of open fields, with three of the immense Muller orphanages to the right and two more in the distance straight ahead. Within ten years, however, the ground was surrounded by dense terraced housing. Thanks to the wisdom of the Graces and the county's many generous backers, the land purchased had space for considerable sporting development. On one side of the pavilion (towards the Nevil Road) there were tennis lawns; on the other (towards an orphanage) bowling greens. Straight ahead, between the far cricket boundary and another orphanage, there was a football pitch complete with its own stands. A cycle track ran round the outside of the cricket field, which soon had a fine Ladies' Pavilion (on the one side of the ground which today lies open), offering a splendid view from the banked, covered seating, high above a ground floor devoted to storage. Seventeen years after his death, Dr Henry's dearest hope had finally been realised.

Today's ground, in the exciting process of major redevelopment, has little that W.G. would recognise other than the Muller orphanages, though these substantial and somewhat sombre buildings having been converted to ordinary residential use. W.G. himself, however, is honoured in several notable ways. First, one of the recently-built apartment blocks that now dominate the far, northern side of the ground is named after him (Gilbert Jessop, Wally Hammond and Tom Graveney being similarly honoured). Then in the completely re-modernised pavilion there is a new Grace Room with a wonderful panoramic view of the cricket and the ability to seat large numbers at major functions. Thirdly, there are the Grace Gates at the Nevil Road entrance, dating back to the centenary celebrations of 1948.

Designed by the club's architect, Thomas Hedley Burrough, the Grace Gates struggle today to make the kind of impact they would have done back in the days of Basil Allen, Charlie Barnett, Jack Crapp, George Emmett and Tom Goddard. Their situation, in a tight corner at the end of a maze of narrow, traffic-clogged roads, is against them, and they open directly onto a modern gym and fitness centre of modest architectural merit. Thomas Burrough had all the right credentials for the job, having been educated at Clifton College and having captained Clifton Sunday 2nds for many years, and it was his happy design for a cast bronze plaque of W.G.

at the wicket, taken from the famous Archibald Stuart Wortley painting, that gives the gates a certain distinction. But 1948 was a time of post-war austerity. This fine tribute, displayed on one of the piers, needs back-up. It would benefit enormously from an appropriate and sympathetic plaque on the other pier to create proper balance. (Perhaps such a plaque might honour other members of the Grace clan, like Teddy, Fred and The Colonel?). But even as the gates are today, in their less than perfect state, they are an integral part of this historically important ground that is now being so impressively modernised. They conjure up images not just of W.G. but of so many other great players, not least, of course, Wally Hammond, who would pass regularly through them in his later years. Bristol's Grace Gates, in their own humble way, are extremely precious.

* * *

W.G.'s new kingdom in 1889 clearly went to his head, bringing out the very worst in him. One morning, furious on arrival to discover some youthful enthusiasts ignoring the 'No Practice Today' signs put up because of bad weather, he weighed in with strong words, met with a cheeky reply, pulled a stump out of the ground and thumped the most argumentative of the young cricketers. The season of 1889 looked likely to get off to the very worst of starts with the county captain charged with assault, but the committee's president managed to calm things down. The incident showed that Agnes, for all her strongly civilising influence, had only been able to achieve so much in sixteen years of marriage.

It would take the Nevil Road wickets some time to settle down, and W.G.s average suffered a little in consequence, yet he still ended the decade strongly, fifth in the averages with 1,396 runs at over 32. He was, perhaps, a little more cautious in 1889. At forty-one he took care to play himself in properly, but his batting was still 'full of its power and judgement', the judgment that 'has kept him easily first for a quarter of a century'. 'His continuing prominence,' continued the *Annual*, 'gives cause for increasing wonder.' He could look back on the 1880s with deep satisfaction. Against the odds, by dint of steely determination and some adroit manoeuvring, he had pulled off the challenge of combining top-class cricket with a part-time medical career.

But just occasionally, in the hush of the night, perhaps, did a recollection of Walter Raleigh Gilbert materialise in sudden vivid flashback amid the shadows of his mind? That occasion, when at sixteen, young Wally had opened the batting with him for a Worcestershire twenty-two? That extraordinary 254 not out Wally made for Teddy's Thornbury? That equally exuberant 205 not out, after they had opened together for I.D. Walker's England eleven at Fenner's? That alarming moment after landing in Western Australia when only a brilliant last-minute ducking of his head had saved him from early extinction from a too-hastily flung boomerang? That impish grin with which he had always somehow managed to placate dear Martha after one of his idiocies? That superb athleticism at deep-leg, which had always made his fielding such an asset to every bowler? That devotion he would always give to his soul-mate Fred, so clearly shown in those last harrowing days at Basingstoke?

And where had he himself been, when The Colonel was down at Basingtoke? Scoring runs in some futile little match? Too busy, too self-centred to drop everything and go to his brother's side? And where, for that matter, had he been at the moment of The Colonel's deepest need? Down at Hove? Keeping his head down? Avoiding the press? Thinking of himself again?

Just occasionally, perhaps, he was more aware of the old weaknesses than the new triumphs.

11

A Tour with Lord Sheffield

Sheffield Park, Melbourne and Hastings, 1890–94

In the Golden Age of the 1890s a new generation of highly talented amateurs, genially presided over by one massive, bearded figure from an older generation and parading like peacocks in colourful blazers and caps, helped elevate an already flourishing sport into a national preoccupation. We are en route to Sheffield Park in Sussex, but are first diverting to the Lord's Museum to take in one small but important piece of Golden Age flamboyance.

In a display cabinet in the lower hall is the gaudy cap worn by W.G. when playing for Lord Sheffield.* Its colours are informative. M.C.C.'s famous red and yellow are blended with purple, which since the days of the Roman emperors has had strong aristocratic associations. The badge, an 'S' picked out in purple and topped by a coronet in red and yellow, further proclaims the patron's pedigree. W.G., we may be sure, would have worn this Golden Age relic with considerable pride.

Henry North Holroyd, the third and last Earl of Sheffield, had in his school days persuaded his father to satisfy his passion for cricket by building him his own ground at their country residence, Sheffield Park. When eventually he inherited the title and the property, in 1876 at the age of forty-four, he so embellished the ground that it became one of the jewels of Golden Age country house cricket. For one shining moment the ultimate in beauty and refinement, it looks out onto the Gothic splendour of Sheffield House, silhouetted romantically against the skies like Arthur's Camelot. Nothing but the best was good enough for Lord Sheffield. Just as the mansion had been re-shaped by James Wyatt and the gardens landscaped by 'Capability' Brown and Humphry Repton, so, too, only the best players were chosen for his elevens and there could not possibly be any other captain than W.G., at least, for the most important fixtures, the occasional first-class matches that regularly featured the Australian tourists and were always enthusiastically embraced by Sussex society.

* * *

We can approach the ground by steam train, like W.G., for the Bluebell Railway enables us to alight at Sheffield Park station that the Third Earl himself opened in 1882 as chairman of the Lewes and East Grinstead Railway Company. Here, in the Golden Age, there were always 'numerous vehicles to pick up passengers and carry them to the ground for a consideration' along a spacious driveway. Meanwhile, the more impecunious spectators, attracted from Brighton by Lord Sheffield's generous insistence on free admission, would set out along a short footpath, cheerfully adorned with flags.

Sheffield House itself is still in private ownership, though now divided into apartments, but the hundred acres of landscape gardens were acquired by the National Trust in 1954 and the surrounding parkland in 2007. Moreover, the Trust in its centenary year of 1995 began the restoration of the old cricket ground that had quite disappeared under a plantation of trees and silt from the lakes. Fourteen years later, it was finally opened. W.G. would have been taken from the mansion by horse and carriage to enter on the far side of the ground, but we will reach it after a brisk walk through the landscape gardens, past brooding lakes and over a dramatic bridge at the Grand Cascade. Having found Queen's Walk, we enter through the trees on our right.

The National Trust, keen to recreate as much of the old atmosphere as possible, made an arrangement with the Armadillos Cricket Club to run the ground and assist in its restoration. A square was laid* and an attractive pavilion in oak created, not unlike the single-storey structure that once served as Lord Sheffield's Players' Pavilion. Today, on permanent display by the pavilion, is the original roller, rescued from a local farm. In W.G.'s day it was pulled across the wicket by a horse wearing leather bootees. Sadly, we can no longer see the Ladies' Pavilion, Lord Sheffield's Pavilion and the Bandstand – three buildings with exquisite wrought ironwork – but the National Trust has erected several informative and well-illustrated information panels with a plan of the ground as it was, so the big occasions in Victorian times are easily re-imagined.

The first time W.G. played here, back in 1883, he is said to have on-driven a six (though perhaps it was actually a hard-run five), the ball soaring 136 yards, high over the carriages of local gentry and spectators sitting four or five deep, before hitting an oak tree, now clearly identified for visitors. The shot was made while W.G. was batting for his own eleven against Lord Sheffield's team during a record stand of 121 with Wally Gilbert.

For Agnes and the wives of other amateurs, the three-day matches at Sheffield House were particularly pleasurable. The octagonal Ladies' Pavilion with its ornamental blue and gold ironwork was suffused with flowers and had a spacious ground-floor drawing room. The walls and ceiling were of light oak, the furniture of walnut, the chaises longues and easy chairs upholstered in green and gold

---

*   On a north–south axis, more satisfactory from a practical point of view than the original east–west one.

velvet. A viewing platform, approached by an elegant spiral staircase, looked out on the wickets, the lakes and the mansion beyond. High quality prevailed everywhere. Even the lavatories and washrooms were fitted with marble, the taps silver-plated. Lord Sheffield's own pavilion likewise had an enclosure for ladies, a tent 'lined with silk' effecting 'a charming little al fresco boudoir'.

While the English professionals and Australian tourists were usually consigned to smart hotels in Brighton and conveyed to and from Sheffield Park station by his Lordship's carriages, the amateurs and their wives stayed at Sheffield House or in the nearby village of Fletching. The mansion's interior, damp and dark, lit only by smoky oil lamps, and with just one bathroom in the entire building, was, for all its ample proportions, in need of modernisation. That W.G. dined some evenings at The Griffin, Fletching, suggests the cooking there was probably more to his liking, but Lord Sheffield certainly did his best to meet W.G.'s insatiable sporting instincts. During one visit in 1890, for example, 'he rose at six o'clock in the morning and spent the forenoon before the game at fishing and shooting. Having made a good score at the match he again resumed his shooting, and finally played a game of billiards before completing the day's sport.'

Though W.G.'s energy was undiminished, these early years of the Golden Age were the least productive in his whole career. In 1890 his 1,476 runs put him eighth in the national averages (at 28.2); the next year, hampered by a wrenched back, a sprained knee and weight of nearly 18 stone, he slumped to 771 runs at 19.76 and a modest 56 wickets. And yet, in the winter of 1891-92, despite this lack of form and fitness, he captained a team in Australia, sponsored and accompanied by Lord Sheffield.

Tours abroad had proliferated since W.G.'s honeymoon visit eighteen years earlier, but were still private ventures, some led by well-connected amateurs, like Lord Harris and the Hon. Ivo Bligh, and others by the shrewd professional trio of Alfred Shaw, Jim Lillywhite and Arthur Shrewsbury. Four years earlier there had been the muddle of two competing teams of visitors: a Shaw-Shrewsbury eleven (linked with Melbourne) and Lord Hawke's team (with Sydney). Lord Sheffield's entry into this confused area of speculation was sparked by a combination of travel lust and the medical advice 'to take a long sea voyage and spend a winter away from England'. There was input, too, from Alfred Shaw who, since retiring from Notts, had been working as cricket manager at Sheffield Park and would travel with the team to Australia in that capacity. For the tour to be welcome there, however, W.G.'s presence was necessary.

Dr Henry and Martha would have been proud of him. He gently turned down Lord Sheffield's first request. Lord Sheffield tried again. W.G. and Agnes were lavishly entertained at Sheffield Park. Walking through the rhododendron bushes by Ten Foot Pond, W.G. and his host looked an oddly matched pair. An Australian newspaper likened the Earl to the kind of a publican to be found in the bush: 'a little, fat stumpy man . . . hair long and straggly, lips and face roughly shaven, and a little fringe of a beard left under the chin, eyes small and cute, thick-necked,

heavy jowled, obstinate, good natured and shrewd.' Living in the era of Oscar
Wilde and taboo-breaking aesthetes, he also dressed with a careless eccentricity.
'He wore an Alpine hat,' wrote another Australian, 'with the colours of his eleven
as a band; dark blue shooting-coat; and roomy, nankeen trousers.'

The visit may well have had its explosive moments, for both men blended
geniality and irascibility in equal measure, but a deal was struck. W.G. would be
paid the huge sum of £3,000 plus all expenses, which the Earl knew would be
considerable, for Shaw had warned him that 'Grace alone would drink enough
wine to sink a ship'. He would also pay for W.G. to be accompanied on the seven-
month tour by Agnes, thirteen-year-old Bessie and nine-year-old Charles, and for a
locum to look after the medical practice. In contrast, eight top-class professionals
would each receive £300. There would be four other amateurs to add tone to
proceedings, one of whom, the outstanding Middlesex and England batsman A.E.
Stoddart, would expect liberal expenses. Cambridge's Gregor MacGregor, Hylton
'Punch' Philipson of Eton and Oxford, and Gloucestershire's Octavius Goldney
Radcliffe would be there more for the fun of it, charming playmates for W.G. on
the long trip.

Everything about the tour was done with style. Lord Sheffield, who loved music
and would always have top-quality brass bands enlivening his big matches, had
arranged for one to play at London's Albert Dock as they embarked in October
1891. There was a cricket net on board ship; the comfort was first-class and Lord
Sheffield proved a munificent host. W.G. was in such high spirits at giving Agnes
and the two children the time of their lives that he even consented to appear in an
evening entertainment, compèring a Christy's Minstrels show.

We can catch up with the tour nearly three months later, at the Oriental Hotel in
Melbourne where, on Christmas Day, W.G. was sitting at a writing-desk, sending
his godfather, William Gilbert Rees in New Zealand, news of their progress.*

My dear William,
    I was very glad to receive your letter and also to know that you are well.
I am afraid there is no chance of our coming to New Zealand as we have
our programme full and shall return to England by the 'Valetta' which sails
at the end of March. Cricket is played out here in a very bad spirit, which
if continued will ruin the game, as after all it is a game of pleasure. Here
everyone suspects his opponents of cheating and trying to best one another.
The umpires are all bad and some are unfair as well...
My wife and two children who are with us are pretty well but do not like
the heat at times. My eldest boy is at Clifton College he is captain of the XI
next year. My second boy, Edgar, is a Naval Cadet. He leaves the Britannia

---

*   The Oriental Hotel was demolished in the early1970s to make way for Collins Place. The letter,
    kindly shared by Rees' great-granddaughter, Rosemary Marryatt, can today be seen in the Lakes
    District Museum, Arrowtown, Central Otago.

now. If we do not see him at 'Malta' on our way home we shall not see him for about three years. My brothers Henry, Ted and Alfred are all well, and old 'Nuncle' Alfred Pocock is as young as ever, he is living with Henry at Kingswood Hill. I will get a book [his autobiography, *Cricket*] for you but have not one at present. I saw George Gilbert at Sydney, he is well but not doing much good I am afraid.

With love from my wife and self to you

    Your loving godson,

    W.G. Grace

At that stage of the tour the team was undefeated after six matches against the odds and three first-class games (in one of which W.G. scored 159 versus Victoria, his only century in 1890–93). As the letter suggests, W.G.'s determination to succeed was as undiminished and confrontational as ever. Indeed, the final eighteen matches over the next three months would be considerably more fraught, coloured by W.G.'s fury over the loss of the first two of the three Test Matches, and W.G. was again to be vilified by an outraged Australian press and public. The confrontations, however, as usual brought out the best in him. Though nearly forty-four, he topped the averages in both the eleven-a-side matches and the minor ones, doing better over the twenty-seven games than fine batsmen like Stoddart, Bobby Abel and Maurice Read.

As regards his family, the now widowed Aunt Caroline was in charge at Thrissell House, keeping an eye on seventeen-year-old Bertie, a day boy at Clifton College, and monitoring the progress of fifteen-year-old Edgar, whose time on a Royal Navy training ship at Dartmouth was culminating in service at sea as a midshipman. Cricket history offers little information about Agnes on the tour, but a reporter, interviewing the team on their return to Plymouth, after noting that W.G. looked bronzed and 'the picture of health', quietly indicated that Agnes may well have often found herself in the role of peace-maker, for her 'kindness and tact throughout the tour have made her even more popular among the members of the team than the Champion himself.' The long itinerary would have had its trials for the family. The hostility and noisy barracking of the big Australian crowds, for example, must have come as quite a shock to the two children as they pored over their scorebooks. It would all have been in strong contrast to the gentle atmosphere at the Gloucestershire home matches.

Agnes would have had important social duties to perform and could hardly have looked after the children the whole time. One possibility is that help was on hand from the Vicar of Fletching's daughter, eighteen-year-old May Attenborough, Lord Sheffield's mistress and probable travelling companion on tour, whom four years later he was to adopt as his daughter and establish as the chatelaine of Sheffield House for the rest of his life. The relationship between the vicar's daughter and the smitten Earl had already caused a local scandal after a series of poison pen letters, emanating from one of the vicar's churchwardens, referred to whoremongery in Sheffield Park. The financial burden of paying for W.G.'s family in Australia would have felt much lighter with the adored May travelling. The outside world would have accepted her happily in the role of governess to the two Grace children. A highly intelligent and accomplished young lady, May was to devote herself for many years to the welfare of the local village children. Her father was a keen cricketer who had played up at the House for some years, and she herself, the year after the tour, started 'Miss May Attenborough's Junior Cricket Club' in Fletching. She was surely an important component of the reclusive Earl's considerable entourage.

* * *

The laconic comment about George Gilbert would have particularly distressed the letter's recipient, for William Gilbert Rees was not only his cousin but also his brother-in-law. Forty years earlier, after delighting Dr Henry and The Mangotsfied with the quality of their cricket, the two had headed off together to make their fortunes in Australia. George's flamboyant cricket had won him great popularity. He had captained New South Wales in the very first inter-colonial match and played, too, against the touring elevens of both H.H. Stephenson and George Parr. But in more recent years he had flitted between jobs, walked out on his wife and large family, and eventually had joined the down-and-outs on the roads with a swag on his back and a billy can in his hand, begging for his keep. Now in his early sixties, with a full beard just like W.G.'s, he had recently returned to Sydney, the scene of many earlier cricketing triumphs, where he hoped he might qualify for occasional handouts.* For W.G. this meeting with his cousin would have been most painful, coming, as it did, only a few years after the problems of George Gilbert's half-brother, Wally Gilbert. W.G. struggled to cope with failure. He was involved in a world of celebrity that demanded success upon success. Compounded failure was something he preferred not to address. Unthinkable. Better left well alone.

* * *

Lord Sheffield's tour revitalised W.G.'s batting. His travels were said to have 'increased his aggressiveness' and in 1892 he was among the best in the country with his 1055 runs averaging 31.02. 'Cricketers everywhere,' commented the magazine *Cricket*, 'were heartily pleased to see the Grand Old Man in full possession of his old and remarkable prowess.' *Lillywhite's Annual*, too, remarked

---

* George Gilbert lay for many years in an unmarked grave at Rookwood Cemetery, Sydney. His great-grandson, Noel Dures, headed a family campaign for a headstone commemorating Gilbert's important role in early Australian cricket. It was unveiled in 2008 by N.S.W.'s Chief Executive Dave Gilbert.

on the 'extraordinary vitality of the Grace brothers': 'W.G., though he is not so brisk in the field and not so deadly with the ball, retains most if not all of the infinite variety which has kept him for nearly thirty years without a superior.'

The season of 1893 went even better. Early on, he found himself back at Sheffield Park, in action against the argumentative and hard-drinking Australian tourists of that year, opening for Lord Sheffield's eleven with the skilful Arthur Shrewsbury. W.G.'s innings of 63 in their record stand of 101 exuded the new aggressiveness. Nine of his fourteen boundaries came from his latest favourite stroke, the late cut. But there was more to the change in his batting than extra aggressiveness. He had altered his technique. In his prime his remarkable eye and timing had allowed him to turn the face of the bat on impact to direct wristy shots into gaps in the field. Now, in his forties, he had made the decision to play straighter and more conventionally, giving the ball the full face of his bat in all his shots in front of the wicket. At the same time, he was more alert than ever for square and late cuts (on the fast grounds of Australia he had made more than a third of his runs cutting) and was emulating the young Prince Ranjitsinhji in developing the leg-glance.

* * *

There were, however, rebellions to be put down in the Gloucestershire committee room, where there was unease that W.G. in his autocratic team selection was over-indulgent towards amateurs and upsetting the few professionals. His son Bertie and (much more talented) godson Charlie Townsend were among the latest young amateur recruits. 'The team did not work harmoniously together,' commented *Wisden*. 'It was quite an open secret that a spirit of mutiny prevailed and matters went so far that at one time a crisis seemed imminent.' The fracas claimed one victim. In 1894 the fifty-four-year-old county secretary, E.M., at last dropped out of the team (though his appearances for Thornbury continued with unabated enthusiasm). A year later the county were to announce a compromise solution: a Selection Committee 'with W.G. Grace allowed the final choice'.

It helped W.G.'s dictatorial cause that in 1894, though his average dropped a little, he was making some big centuries, taking 196 off Cambridge University at Lord's and 139 at Fenner's. Against the touring South Africans, moreover, he scored 129 not out at Bristol and also took 9-71 in one innings.

* * *

The Priory Meadow Shopping Centre, said to be 'Hastings' number one shopping destination', is a late twentieth-century redevelopment of the much-loved Central Cricket and Recreation Ground, where W.G. played over forty games and, in 1894 during the Hastings Festival in September, claimed his 98th first-class century, batting for the Gentlemen against the Players. It was a ground he had enjoyed ever since a double century for the United South back in 1874.

The new shopping centre has a sculpture by Allan Sly called 'The Spirit of Cricket', a ten-foot high bronze of a young player on one leg after hooking a ball wildly towards fine-leg. The ball is lodged on the wall of a nearby shop. An inscription below the statue (commissioned by Boots and unveiled by Her Majesty the Queen in June 1997) acknowledges, without any obvious sense of embarrassment, that cricket had been enjoyed on the site for over a hundred and thirty years. The River Island store marks the approximate position of the wickets where W.G. gave the people and visitors of Hastings so much enjoyment. Alas, no statue, however striking, can be consolation for the loss of this lovely and historic ground. Film survives of its demolition. One last sweeping, panoramic view of the ground is particularly moving, shot just before the bulldozers moved in, with poignant cries of alarm from the Hastings seagulls at the impending vandalism of their town's history.

The 1894 Festival match began inauspiciously with a late start – W.G. had been partridge shooting at Cambridge – but his arrival at the main gate with Billy Murdoch 'in a ramshackle four-wheeler' was spotted by his future biographer Clifford Bax, then a young, awestruck schoolboy: 'A huge man with twinkling eyes and a great bushy beard got out of the cab, lugging after him a capacious cricket-bag.' With his 'square bowler hat' the great W.G. looked like 'a prosperous farmer'.

The ninety-eighth century itself was a steady affair, 131 runs in 220 minutes, but then the Players' attack of Mold, Lockwood, Peel, J.T. Hearne and Martin was a very fine one, and he weighed nineteen stone and was slow between the wickets. Match reports suggest that when the ball was there to be hit, he could still respond massively. Half-volleys were struck hard and straight, along the ground or on the up, with a flash of the mighty forearms. From the sea end he drove Hearne right out of the ground, the ball landing at the front door of the Prince's Hotel in South Terrace. When Mold, a fast bowler whose highly suspect action was eventually outlawed, repeatedly pitched menacingly short, the nonchalant W.G. kept hooking him with turned wrists for 2 to deep square-leg. His cutting was, as ever, highly productive. 'His famous stroke just out of reach of cover-point,' wrote one watcher, 'was repeated, again and again'. The gentle leg-glance was likewise utilised, even the slow Bobby Peel being glanced for 4, and so, too, the late cut, Jack Hearne's medium-paced off-cutters being dispatched that way to the boundary on several occasions.

W.G. batted with eight partners, one of whom was Bertie, who spent thirty minutes scoring just 4 (though at their next game together, at the Reigate Festival, Bertie was for once to outscore his father with 148 not out). W.G.'s 131 was all the more impressive in that it was made on a drying wicket on which the Players (boasting Gunn, Abel, Brockwell and Alec Hearne) had just been bowled out for 85.

* * *

The picturesque Fletching Church lies close to one of Sheffield House's lodge gates. Attached to the church is a small mausoleum, created by James Gibbs for the first Lord Sheffield. Huge crowds were to gather around it in May 1909 as the seventy-seven-year-old Third Earl was laid to rest with his ancestors. W.G. was not there, but from his time on tour in Australia he knew the chief mourner well enough, the Earl's adopted daughter May Attenborough. Though the title had become extinct and the estate was to be sold as there were no male heirs, May's future had been assured with the gift of a large house in the village. She had no intention, however, of spending the rest of her life in widow's weeds. Clearly a very spirited lady, she married twice and ended her days in Fiji.

Fletching church has a fine stained-glass window in memory of May's father, a public tribute from the Earl to his old, amenable vicar, and a private gift of love to the vicar's daughter. Just outside the church's entrance porch, we can admire the striking sculpture Lord Sheffield insisted on providing for the grave of May's father and mother, and pay one final salute to the love-struck Earl whose generosity and passion for cricket were much to the advantage of W.G.

12

A National Treasure

The Golden Indian Summer, 1895–98

Soon after the Hastings match, towards the end of 1894, the Graces moved home. The long lease on Thrissell House had finally expired, and its owner, who lived next door at 59 and may not have been enamoured of the cricket net, had made it clear he would not be renewing it. Even though the new home, 15 Victoria Square, Clifton, was almost two miles away, W.G. continued to work from his surgery in Thrissell Lodge, which he had acquired a few years earlier (number 55 on the corner of Thrissell Street).

Victoria Square was very different from grimy Stapleton Road and much more in keeping with W.G.'s celebrity status. Created in the 1840s on Lansdown Road, it was enclosed by three grand terraces in highly ornamented style, each designed to look more like a palace than a collection of individual houses. The Graces' double-fronted, end-of-terrace home gave them more space, though the small triangular garden at the side and back offered little scope for cricket. For Agnes and Aunt Caroline there was the convenience of an adjacent archway that led directly to the Clifton Arcade and the shops of Regent Street. Clifton College and Clifton Down railway station were both half-a-mile away.

Today a blue plaque on 15 Victoria Square announces that 'Dr W.G. Grace the cricketer lived here, 1894–96'. The square is much as it was then, though many of the houses, including the Graces', have been subdivided into flats. Students and tourists abound. The central gardens, no longer the private haven of the 1890s, are a popular recreational area, and there is an almost continental atmosphere in the little street-market in Boyce's Avenue, just through the arch, where the open-air tables of the Primrose Café do good business.

* * *

The striking improvement in life-style that the move to Victoria Square gave W.G. was mirrored in his cricket. He was now forty-seven, but 1895 proved a wonderful season, the aggregate of 2,346 runs at an average of 51.00 being one of the highest in his whole career and including no less than nine centuries. It began in mid-April with a return to Downend for a pre-season warm-up on a ground across the road from Clematis House and adjacent to Christ Church, where, only two months earlier, he and the family had said a sorrowful farewell to his sister Alice Bernard. He would rather not have been reminded of this so soon, but had made a promise to his brother-in-law John Dann that he would bring a county eleven to play an Eighteen of Downend to celebrate the ground that the Christ Church vicar had finally, after much endeavour, been able to conjure up from a rented grazing field.

* * *

It was a moving experience for W.G. to be batting a hundred yards away from The Chesnuts; across the road from Downend House and Clematis; and in the shadow of Christ Church. The match had started well. The Downend Eighteen had been bowled out for 62, thanks to his latest protégé, Gilbert Jessop. He was now at the wicket, enjoying being back in the countryside where his parents had spent so many happy years together, delighting in the large crowd that he had attracted, and determined to give his dear brother-in-law good value for money.

He was three not out and facing Edwin 'Ted' Biggs, a burly carpenter and the Downend captain. W.G. knew his mother Mary well. She ran the post-office-cum-grocery just past Downend House. So he'd treat young Ted with respect; he'd be careful not to wreck his confidence and upset his mother.

Ted Biggs had grown up in awe of W.G. and his brothers. When Martha Grace was still alive, they'd been pointed out to him by his parents as perfect examples of filial devotion. 'If there is a concert, one of them takes her. If there is a meet of the hounds, they see she is at it in her pony-carriage. If the ice bears on the old quarry, they get her in a chair and push it about in front of them as they skate. That's how a son treats a mother, Ted.' As he reached the end of his long run, Ted tried to put all thoughts of plump Mrs Grace away from him and concentrate on the task in hand. It was marvellous that the Reverend had persuaded the Grand Old Man to bring across such a fine team. A great day for Downend! Approaching the wicket that he himself had helped prepare, emptying buckets of water over it during the preceding week, Ted increased his considerable pace, pivoted himself on his right leg, aimed his left shoulder at the bearded figure and hurled his arm over.

He hadn't of course meant to bowl a leg-break. The Downend pitch was, as yet, unpredictable, despite the Reverend's best efforts with the roller. But a fine leg-break it was. There were gasps of disappointment from all round the ground. Ted Biggs had clean bowled the Champion.

* * *

There's a plaque at the cricket ground in Downend, on the older of its two pavilions, unveiled by W.G.'s sister Blanche Dann in 1922 and commemorating a joyful occasion: 'This pavilion was erected and the cricket ground purchased by supporters of Downend cricket club in memory of the world's greatest cricketer,

Dr W.G. Grace.' The future of the W.G. Grace Memorial Ground, however, looks insecure. The club's present ambitions for expansion are inhibited by the lack of space, and, despite a petition of nearly seven hundred local people urging that the land should not be given over to building development, the club's members have voted to explore that avenue as a first step to securing a new ground. One must hope, even at this late stage, that other ways can be found to accommodate the club's ambitions.* The loss of the Revd Dann's little gem of a ground would both betray those who bought it specifically as a public tribute to W.G., and, at the same time, surrender an absolutely central part of Downend's unique collection of Grace mementoes and memorials.

* * *

Two days after the Downend match W.G. was in sparkling form at Nevil Road, making an unbeaten century against Bertie and twenty-three other Colts of Gloucestershire, and, in his initial first-class game of the season, captaining M.C.C. against Sussex at Hove, he surprised everyone. Though he was as big as ever, nearing twenty stone, he was at last free from his nagging knee problems and it was making a big difference. The old certainty on the front foot had returned. Word went round that W.G., in scoring his ninety-ninth first-class century, was a reincarnation of his old self.

A week later, in mid-May, the county ground was full for the first home match of the season, the visit of Somerset. Indeed, the whole nation was waiting expectantly, eager to celebrate the Champion's hundred 100s. Friends and family abounded. Agnes was there, of course, with Bessie. So, too, brothers Henry, Alfred and Teddy, who, along with uncle Alfred and Methven Brownlee, devotedly followed every ball of the game, 'restless as schoolboys'. Somerset were dismissed for 303, W.G. bowling unchanged throughout the afternoon to take 5-87 in forty-five five-ball overs. The spring sunshine had given way to a biting chill by 5.50 p.m. and there were even said to be a few snowflakes in W.G.'s beard, as, opening the innings, he faced up to Sammy Woods, the Somerset captain. Woods, then in his late twenties, was an archetypal Golden Age amateur: public school-educated, a sporting hero at Cambridge, a brave England rugby union forward, an all-smiling cricketing all-rounder of immense heart, whose yorkers and well-disguised slower balls were to gain him a thousand wickets. In contrast, at the other end, there was the slow left-arm of Edwin 'Ted' Tyler, one of the Somerset professionals. Forty minutes were left. A piercing wind cut across Ashley Down but the wicket was still hard and good. Hopes remained high, even when two wickets fell cheaply. W.G.'s new partner was young Charlie Townsend, almost as tall as W.G. and as thin as his partner was bulky. Thrice W.G. on-drove Tyler for four, one shot landing on the

* Aware of its important Grace heritage, Downend Cricket Club was playing home and away matches with E.M.'s Thornbury in the summer of 2015, to mark the centenary of W.G.'s death.

newly laid cycle track. Twice he dispatched Sammy Woods to the leg-side ropes. A brisk partnership ended the day brightly day with Gloucestershire 58 and W.G. 32. One question was on all lips. Might tomorrow be the day?

It brought no dazzling Golden Age sunshine. Instead, an overcast sky lowered over the packed ground, swept by a cold northerly breeze, but nobody seemed to worry, as W.G. resumed with Charlie Townsend. Runs flowed. Woods tried all his bowlers, but within two hours of flawless batting the score had reached 181-2. The scoreboard gave no further details, but many on the ground had been making count. One of the younger onlookers later wrote of this moment: 'Sam Woods, great-hearted sportsman if ever there was one, who was bowling, turned round and looked at the scoring box. One of the scorers leaned out and held up two fingers. Sam ran slowly up to the wicket and delivered a full toss on the leg-side and the master, getting the ball in the middle of the bat, hit it safely and surely to the boundary. There was a wild outburst of cheering; all who had seats rose; hats and caps were waved; all the Somerset men joined in the applause, whilst the hero of the momentous event turned to each side of the ground and raised the peak of his M.C.C. cap.' Champagne was rushed out from the pavilion. 'I would have given a year of my life,' sighed Teddy over the uproar to Henry, 'almost anything, to have been out there with him when he made that hit.'

The crowd settled down. Everyone knew W.G. He wouldn't throw it all away now, and, of course, he didn't. A couple of wickets fell, but he kept going at an astonishing rate. His 200 arrived and, with it, another Jereboam. More wild cheering. More concentration, too, as the crowd settled. W.G. would surely not yet rest content. And so it proved. It was not until just after 5 o'clock when, with his score at 288, he was the ninth man out after misjudging a drive to the long-off boundary, where Tyler, jumping high, held a fine, one-handed catch.

* * *

We are at the county ground, Nevil Road, looking down from high-up in the newly rebuilt pavilion at the very arena where the runs and champagne flowed so freely that special day in May 1895. A Heritage Trust is currently fund-raising for a new Museum and Learning Centre that will display again the many Grace mementoes the county possesses. So Gloucestershire's archivist, Roger Gibbons, has kindly brought along one or two particularly relevant items.

Amazingly, the ball that W.G. hit for 288 survives. When the tenth wicket of the Gloucestershire innings fell, Ted Tyler raced off in the direction of the fielder who had made the catch, caught up with him on the pavilion steps, persuaded him to let him have the ball and saved it for posterity. After the hard time it had had, the ball is just a little out of shape with its seam totally worn down. Tyler would have achieved little spin from it in that condition. A later owner had a band of silver attached to it, inscribed 'W G Grace Hundredth 100 c. Tyler b Woods 9th out (288)'.

There before us, too, is the actual bat that scored the hundredth 100. Made by Nicolls, it is light to handle with an easy pick-up. Levi James Nicolls was a young Sussex carpenter who had started making cricket bats in the village of Robertsbridge in the 1880s and whose firm was to merge with another and become Gray-Nicolls in 1940. The bat's surface is quite cracked and necessitated some binding. A small brass plate states that it was presented to the county by W.G.'s grandson, Commander Edgar Grace, in 1948 on the centenary of his birth.

W.G. had acquired the bat* at Hastings (not far from the Nicolls factory at Robertsbridge) during his ninety-eighth century. He had spotted it in the lunch interval in a cabinet with several other new bats, expressed a liking for it, been given it and used it to complete that innings of 131. It was to last him for much of the 1895 season, including the new triumph of being the first player to score 1,000 runs in May, as the ink inscription in his own hand on the back of the heavily varnished bat proclaims:

W.G. Grace
1895
With this bat
I scored 1,000 runs
between May 9 and May 30
in 1895.
May 9.10.11 at Lords, M.C.C.
v Sussex 13 & 103
May 13.14.15 at Lords, M.C.C.
v Yorkshire 18 & 25
May 16.17.18 at Bristol, Gloucester
v Somerset 288
May 20.21.22 at Cambridge, Gentlemen
of England v Cambridge Univ. 52
May 23.24.25 at Gravesend,
Gloucester v Kent 257 & 73 not
May 27.28.29 at The Oval, England
v Surrey 18
May 30 at Lords, Gloucester
v Middlesex 169

Events that year took on a dreamlike quality as success mounted on success. One highlight was taking the family to Lord's to support Bertie in that jewel in London society's season, the University Match. Doing his very best to live up to the name of W.G. Grace jnr. and backed up by some embarrassingly loud paternal support,

* The archive at the current Gray-Nicolls premises includes a letter of October 1895 in which W.G. endorses the bat with a mention of its twin achievements. 'So I think I may call it my record bat.'

the admirably determined Bertie had just scraped into the Cambridge team. For W.G., with his susceptibility to varsity glamour, it was a thrilling occasion. Dressed with meticulous and unaccustomed attention to detail, resplendent in frock coat and silk top and unaware of the smiles he was raising on many sides, the rubicund W.G. strode around Lord's, family in train, like some visiting potentate out to make the biggest impression of all at a royal jubilee, and his pride swelled to new heights when, against most people's expectation, Bertie scored a creditable 40.

During the afternoon Charles Green, Essex cricket's supremo and the prosperous Director of the Orient Steam Navigation Company, had invited W.G. to his well-appointed box. Later in the afternoon, when Green returned after circulating for a while elsewhere, he was shocked to discover his champagne disappearing in large quantities as a large company, invited there by W.G., toasted Bertie's success with enthusiasm. In the surreal atmosphere of 1895 W.G. was in danger of losing touch with reality.

* * *

The third memento from the Nevil Road archive, a Coalport bone china dessert plate, reflects this. In the bizarre aftermath to W.G.'s twin achievements of May 1895, national rejoicing, fanned by the ever more influential press, took on extraordinary proportions. A spate of dinners in W.G.'s honour were held and all manner of souvenirs were produced for an avid public. A Coalport plate was typical, with a central image of W.G. from which ninety stumps and ten bats radiated with details of the hundred centuries. The *Daily Telegraph* was soon announcing a Testimonial Fund, encouraging members of the public each to contribute one shilling. M.C.C. and Gloucestershire, who both might reasonably have expected to take the lead in any such gesture of generosity, responded by creating funds of their own in conjunction with the *Daily Telegraph*'s Testimonial. The joint total came to a remarkable £9,073 8s 3d, well over half a million in modern money. Nobody seemed to care in the euphoria of the moment quite where it left W.G.'s amateur status, and *Wisden* coyly quoted from Shakespeare that 'nice customs curtsy to great kings'.

The plate before us is a special one, a reminder of the sudden wealth that had come W.G.'s way. Among the many dinners he had enjoyed in the summer of 1895 was one given by the Century Club, a Bristol group that included accountants, solicitors, a builder and contractor, an official receiver in bankruptcy and the owner of a wine and spirits company, though the most prominent was surely Methven Brownlee. In January 1896 W.G., in munificent mood, decided to host a return fixture, and, now that money was no object, he asked Coalport to produce eighteen special plates detailing the hundred 100s, one for each person at the dinner. These had the distinctive feature of his own signature as the bold central image and, on the back of the plates, the table plan of the dinner with the names of the eighteen participants.

Such dinners were usually all-male affairs, but Agnes found herself invited occasionally. She was present, for example, in February 1896, when the county made a presentation of their collection towards the Testimonial Fund at a dinner at the Clifton Club in Bristol's Pall Mall, a gathering of seventy guests, presided over by the Duke of Beaufort, and full of familiar family faces (with the sad exception of Henry Grace, who had died suddenly a few months earlier). W.G. was given a gold watch with a W.G. monogram and Agnes received a beautifully engraved silver kettle*, complete with a silver heating device underneath, mounted on four elegant legs. W.G. was deeply moved by the lovely gift to Agnes, but struggled for words. 'But for my wife's help,' he said eventually, 'I would not have done as well as I have in cricket.'

* * *

The Indian Summer continued in 1896. At forty-eight W.G. averaged nearly 43 for his 2,135 runs, scoring four centuries and even managing 52 wickets. Sussex were plundered for 243 at Brighton and 301 at Bristol. He was still captaining England against the Australians as a matter of course. That year the Australian fast bowler, Ernest Jones, famously sent a ball through W.G.'s beard at Sheffield Park. In fact, according to Stanley Jackson who was batting at the other end, it went flying past him, head high, and over wicket-keeper Jim Kelly to the boundary:

> This was the ball about which the Beard Story originated. I can see W.G. now. He threw his head back, which caused his beard to stick out. Down the pitch went W.G., stroking his beard, to Harry Trott and said: 'Here, what is all this?' And Trott said: 'Steady, Jonah.' To which Jones made that famous remark: 'Sorry, Doctor, she slipped.'

* * *

Victoria Square was no longer satisfactory for a doctor of means. The garden was much too small and lacked any privacy. W.G. hankered for spacious grounds, like those at dear Chesnuts, or even better. So when a large, sprawling home of the 1850s became vacant within a five-minute walk of the county ground, W.G. seized it eagerly. Ashley Grange, an architectural oddity, a merging of two attached houses, one of two floors and the other of three, was impressively large, ideal for a big man with ambitions to match. In grounds that lay between Ashley Down Road and the newly built terraces of Sefton Park Road, it offered a great deal: rooms galore for themselves, Aunt Caroline and as many guests as they might ever wish to invite; a curving drive that ended up in a circular sweep in front of the house; an ample stable and yard; spacious lawns and colourful gardens at the back

---

*   The kettle and stand were purchased by M.C.C. in 1983.

with attractive views to St Bartholomew's Church; and an orchard that absolutely dwarfed the old one at Downend.

In living so close to the county ground that, only six years earlier, he and E.M. had discovered and secured, W.G. was firming up his right to rule. At forty-eight he felt far from ready to step down from his kingdom. Indeed, any committee members who thought he should do so would discover how wide of the mark they were. Dr Grace of Ashley Grange was in a more naturally dominant position that Dr Grace of Victoria Square in far-away Clifton. Indeed, he must have felt supreme and unchallengeable.

* * *

As we walk from the former orphanages along Ashley Down Road, in the direction of the town, we can pick out occasional houses that survive from W.G.'s day, when, instead of today's flow of noisy traffic, the only encroachment on the Ashley Down stillness were the occasional horse-drawn vehicles, the crocodiles of orphan girls in their bonnets and shawls and that *rara avis* of the ultra-rich, quite unsuited to the hills of Bristol, the experimental motor car. The most important landmark for us, on our right, is Ashley House, the home of a former Bristol mayor, the stone piers of whose entrance gates, elaborately decorated with banded rustication, also survive. An old Ordnance Survey map shows the Graces' Ashley Grange a little further down the hill from Ashley House, its next door neighbour, and just a little further away from the main road. Ashley House, though fractionally smaller than the Graces' home, gives an idea of the considerable visual impact it must have made, high on a hill, with wonderful views of Ashley Dale. Ashley Grange was, alas, knocked down in 1936, after a period as a nursing home, all of its grounds being covered by the modern housing of Williamson Road and beyond. A local historian has written of one small relic, the name of the house 'on a block of stone near the base of a silver birch tree', but, if it still survives, it frustratingly eluded us.

* * *

As W.G. approached fifty, Grace-mania mounted and the excellent form continued. In 1897, a year that began inauspiciously with the death of Uncle Alfred*, he averaged virtually 40 from his 1,532 runs. He was still taking some wickets and 'still the backbone of the Gloucestershire eleven'. His average in 1898 for a similar aggregate mounted to 42 and that year he captained Gloucestershire to a most creditable third position in championship, which now embraced fourteen counties.

---

*   Uncle Alfred had remained W.G.'s most devoted supporter and critic into his eighties, a regular at all the county's home games. 'He usually walked from the enclosure to the pavilion at the close of each innings,' wrote an obituarist, 'his bent figure and white hair making him conspicuous'. He had ended his days with the Danns at the Downend vicarage.

The country was in jubilee mood. A year before, there had been the euphoria of Queen Victoria's Diamond Jubilee, a time for taking stock of nationhood and pride in empire. Now the taking stock and the pride had turned to the country's sporting champion.

Two matches in July 1898 became a crucial part of this legendary Golden Jubilee summer. The first took place at Leyton, where Essex, one of the new additions to the championship, were entertaining Gloucestershire. The match was riddled with bad temper, most of it generated by W.G., who, in bowling Essex out for 128 had taken 7-44. His gamesmanship, however, had gone down very badly. Several of the seven wickets were contentious, including a very doubtful caught and bowled:

Some of the Essex batsmen, dismissed by Grace, had sauntered very angrily pavilion-wards. Perrin returned in a fury. He had spooned up an easy chance, but Grace was slow to move to it and caught the ball very low down. To many it seemed that Grace caught the ball on the half volley. He, however, clinched Perrin's departure with the triumphant cry, 'Not bad for an old 'un!' Perrin appealed to the umpire, whose view had been obscured by Grace, as usual. He appealed in vain. Gilbert Jessop, in a good position at cover-point to see what had happened, was adamant that Grace had caught the ball on the first bounce… (Meredith, *The Demon and the Lobster*)

Bad feeling intensified when W.G. pinned up in the Leyton pavilion a congratulatory telegram he had received from Bristol saying, 'How cruel of you to bowl the rabbits out!'

Thoroughly irritated, as W.G. intended them to be, the Essex team tried too hard in the field, particularly the demon fast bowler Charles Kortright, who grew more and more furious at the careless way Grace ignored the many direct hits on his body and cut his fierce deliveries with nonchalance through the slips in a quite brilliant innings of 126. Matters came to a head when Gloucestershire were set 148 to win. Two wickets fell quickly and Essex thought W.G. should have followed, caught and bowled by Walter Mead, but W.G. claimed the ball had bounced and the umpire eventually agreed. Kortright thereupon submitted him to a barrage of short-pitched deliveries from one of which W.G. was dropped in the slips. As W.G. passed Kortright, remonstrating with the poor fielder as everyone returned to the pavilion at close of play, W.G. could not resist a quick word. 'Cheats never prosper,' he muttered darkly.

The next morning Gloucestershire pulled off a one-wicket win, largely thanks to a brave innings from W.G. that ended in some legendary repartee:

Fresh from a night's rest, Kortright was swooping in like a Fury. Sewell was caught off a skier. Townsend's off-stump was sent spinning. And Grace himself, who had reached 49, was bowled. Two balls earlier Kortright had beaten him outside the off stump. The Doctor had snicked, Tom Russell had clung on and the fielders jumped in triumph. But the umpire stayed unmoved. This time, however, there could be no doubt. The leg stump was uprooted, rearing high in the air before coming down to rest seven yards back. The middle stump was uprooted, too. The Doctor made his usual dumb-show of astonishment and then began to walk away. 'Surely, you're not going, doctor,' said Kortright, half smiling, half snarling. 'There's one stump standing.' (*ibid.*)

* * *

The scene of the acrimonious confrontation between Grace and Kortright was a ground where cricket has been played for well over two hundred years. It was purchased by Essex in 1888, when their chairman and captain, Charles Green, was pushing hard to point his county towards first-class status, and a wooden pavilion was erected shortly afterwards, funded by an appeal for £3,500. Its design was suitably grand, to match the county's ambitions, its pebble-dash and mock-Tudor timber reflecting the Leyton of the times, a growing suburban town of thirty thousand, home to commuting city clerks, lower-grade civil servants and local traders. Though Essex last played at Leyton in 1977, the ground is still to be found close by Leyton Midland Road station, and there is even optimistic talk of an Essex return one day via Twenty20. For the moment it is home to Leyton Cricket Club, schools and community groups. Though anxieties have been voiced about longstanding feuds between gangs frequenting the area, it has proved a good venue for big events like the Jamaica 50th Independence Day which united Jamaicans and other residents in a happy multicultural celebration, and Family Weekend Festivals, often featuring the Waltham Forest Caribbean Carnival. The pavilion where W.G. posted his provocative telegram shows its years but is Grade II listed.

* * *

Nine days after the match at Leyton ended, the Lord's pavilion was the central witness to the conclusion of the Grace-Kortright feud. It is an exact contemporary of Leyton's pavilion, having been opened in 1889, as if in readiness for the Golden Age that Grace's great feats had brought to pass. Jubilee joy was at its height. The traditional date of the annual Gentlemen v. Players fixture had been deliberately put back a week so that it could open on 18 July, W.G.'s fiftieth birthday. County secretaries had also agreed that no other fixtures should take place on the same days, so that the teams could be at fullest strength. It became the single most memorable game of cricket's Golden Age. Though still suffering from an injured heel and hand (war wounds from Leyton), W.G. arrived at Lord's with Agnes and Bessie at eleven o'clock on his birthday morning beaming like a bearded cherub.

Lord's was en fête on 18 July 1898. Long before the start, spectators formed a long queue outside the gates. Cabs were arriving by the dozen. The mid-summer heat was already so intense that several roads were blocked by hansoms, their horses collapsed with fatigue within the shafts. The ground was full by 11.30 a.m. but a few thousand more were allowed in, to squat on the ground in front. Straw-hatted men formed the majority, but lady enthusiasts thronged the long covered stand adjacent to the pavilion. There were over twenty thousand in the ground, but it was an orderly crowd. The only time the police were called into action was when a gentleman in the grand stand disregarded the sign 'No Smoking' and was forcibly ejected ... When W.G. took a stroll on the north side of the ground to visit the telegraph office, he was accompanied by tremendous bursts of applause. Everywhere he was confronted by a sea of smiling faces, a channel of outstretched hands. W.G. himself is said to have smiled non-stop for three whole days ... (*ibid.*)

The gleaming red-brick pavilion, just nine years old, made for a real sense of theatre as W.G, with the next ten best amateurs behind him, strode down the staircase, through the swirl of enthusiasts in the Long Room, and passed between the impressive array of top hats on the members' benches. He was greeted, as he emerged on the field of play, by a standing ovation all around the ground; a huge outburst of cheering and screaming; a violent waving of hats, newspapers, handkerchiefs and whatever else came to hand. For the crowd were not just cheering W.G. They were applauding a symbol of continuity; resistance to the ravages of time and change; and the indestructible nature of their own values, society and empire. The delirious reception lasted all the way to the wicket.

His opening bowler, Charles Kortright, might have arrived at the ground with an unsettled score or two, but how can one scowl for long at a smiling bearded cherub? Animosity unfroze. Kortright came pounding in for his skipper off his full thirty strides and bowled devotedly all morning. The game moved on. Scores really didn't matter. All that counted was The Old Man. So when he came out to bat, though very lame, pandemonium again broke out. It took him time to find his touch, and Lord's watched breathless. But then, uproar, as he off-drove Jack Hearne for 2, drove him to the ladies' seats on the onside for 4, and hit him to leg for 2, all in the same over. Soon, too, there came a magnificent pull that sent the ball high over the heads of the spectators, over a carriage and pair and onto a hotel terrace. He was out for 43, but the crowd stood to him.

Eventually the Gentlemen were left with 296 to win and less than two and a half hours' play. W.G. had been struck on the wrist by a rising ball in his first innings and was not expected to bat. But when the score was 77-7, out he came. He was cheered from the moment he limped down the steps to the pavilion gate to the moment he removed one bail, as was his custom, took guard and made his mark with it. Two more wickets fell quickly. The jubilee match looked like ending in inglorious defeat, when, at 80-9, Kortright joined him. For seventy minutes there was a thrilling contest as the two antagonists at Leyton fought their way towards the honourable draw that would be theirs at 7.00 p.m. They had nearly doubled the score when Kortright fell, in the very last over, driving too ambitiously, leaving W.G. undefeated on 31. It had been that kind of heroic fight against the odds that so ennobles the game. W.G. delightedly slipped his arm into Kortright's as they approached the cheering pavilion. The reconciliation was complete. The crowd milled around the pavilion, calling for their heroes and cheering them to the echo. W.G.'s jubilee match had ended as gloriously as it had begun. As ever, the great batsman had given his devoted admirers value for money.

A small clip of moving film survives of the two teams at lunchtime on W.G.'s birthday, passing the camera two-by-two rather self-consciously, a Gentleman beside a Player:

> Little conversation is taking place between the two sides. The captains, Grace and Shrewsbury, leading the parade, are within shot for the longest and neither exchanges a word with the other. Grace himself looks cheerful and moves comparatively easily. He is the only cricketer to play up to the camera. As he approaches, he doffs his cap at the bioscope, grinning conspiratorially... (*ibid.*)

* * *

There was good cause for a conspiratorial grin on that great day, for the cricket world was in for a major surprise. In the autumn of 1898, at the height of Grace-mania, with the nation clamouring for a knighthood, W.G. upped and left Bristol and re-settled his family in London. It was not a sudden decision, but something he had been pondering some time, and the complete truth behind it may probably never be fully revealed. One thing is certain. W.G. had lost his sense of balance amid the delirium of the nation. Rich and fêted beyond his wildest hopes, magically re-finding his touch as a cricketer and enjoying an unprecedentedly golden Indian Summer in his late forties, he had much to feed his ego and throw him off balance. Roman generals, enjoying a triumph in the forum and the acclaim of the masses after a successful military campaign, used to have a slave standing at the back of the chariot whispering, 'Remember you are only human'. Agnes, this time, seems not to have been standing there at the back of the triumphal car in the role of helpful servant.

The move from Bristol was precipitated by an offer from the company that ran Crystal Palace, the famous Exhibition Centre and Park, to create, manage and captain there a London County Cricket Club. The job, that would start in 1899, would earn him more than £1,000 a year. He didn't need such big money any more. He didn't even need to be a doctor. He could live off the shrewdly invested proceeds of the Testimonial of 1895. But the kingship of Ashley Down, that had always had its drawbacks thanks to a few dissenters in the county committee, could now be augmented by the kingship of Crystal Palace, one of the most glitteringly famous places in the whole country. He would live in London and rule both kingdoms. He would be closer, too, to those other two kingdoms, Lord's and The Oval, which, though of course he could never actually own, would always be his dearest allies and immensely welcoming.

Winners write their own history. So over the years W.G.'s move to London and the subsequent break with Gloucestershire have been passed over with a regretful word or two without much suggestion that there could have been some hidden agenda. But there is one further Grace memento at Nevil Road, stored away until the creation of the new museum, that opens up a mystery which, just possibly, played its part in the whole muddled saga of the move away from Bristol.

13

A Short Retrospection

The Harriet Fowler Mystery

The memento in question is an armchair thought to have been used by W.G. himself in his earlier, less weighty years. Re-upholstered in a light green, the small padded tub chair was presented to Gloucestershire around fifty years ago by the descendants of Harriet Fowler, a Herefordshire spinster who was with the Graces, as cook and general help, from the early days in Stapleton Road to the later excitements of Victoria Square and Ashley Grange. It was part of the furniture in Harriet's room when she first arrived and was gifted to her at the conclusion of her service, at around the time of the move to London.

The Fowler family's historian, Ken Clarke, remembers that, when he first saw the chair, back around 1950, he was extremely startled at being told that Harriet, his great-grandmother's sister, had born two children to W.G. 'We have never seen any proof of this, but my mother and my aunts believed it firmly.' One child is well documented. In December 1869, the twenty-four-year-old Harriet gave birth to (Frances) Emily Fowler. Little Emily was brought up by Harriet's sister Ann Hill, a glove-maker, as one of the Hills' own large family, but she always knew who her real mother was. The second child is more of a mystery. 'My family insisted that Harriet had also had a boy,' writes Ken Clarke, 'but we have found no trace of him. However, an elderly cousin stated categorically that when Emily went to her mother's funeral in 1912, she was spoken to by 'her brother' who up to that time had been unknown to her. My mother, Ann Hill's granddaughter, believed that this boy had been brought up as 'a gentleman' by the Grace family, but as yet there is no clear evidence to back up the story.'

W.G. would have been in his early twenties at the time of this suggested liaison. His cricketing and social commitments certainly brought him from time to time not far from Harriet's home, the village of Munsley near Ledbury. Worcester, for example, where his aunt Rose and cousin Wally Gilbert lived, he knew very well. In 1868 he was playing there with the United South against a Twenty-two of Worcestershire that included the Earl of Coventry and two of the influential Lytteltons. In 1870 he was opening with Wally for the Twenty-two Gentlemen of Worcestershire (alongside Lord Somerset and the Marquess of Queensbury) against the United North. Ross-on-Wye was even nearer Munsley. W.G. had first played there in 1866 with his father's West Gloucestershire eleven. In 1871 he and Fred were back enjoying a pre-season frolic for Ross-on-Wye against Weston (Fred scoring a quick 174 and W.G. 93). Two days later W.G. Grace's Ross Eleven played G.F. Grace's. Clearly his contacts in the area were considerable.

The wildness of the young Graces and the atmosphere of that early tour to North America encourage an open-minded response to the Fowler family legend. Two questions arise. Why did Harriet Fowler leave Munsley to join the Graces in Bristol? And why, twenty years later, did she return?

There seems no obvious answer to the first question. Harriet, daughter of a Herefordshire blacksmith, was to spend the whole of her life, with the exception of her time with the Graces, within a fifteen-mile radius of the village where she was born. She had little education and fewer prospects. But the birth of her two children changed her lifestyle dramatically. She had been working beforehand as a maid on a small farm. But by the mid-1870s she was cook and housekeeper to an elderly couple, the Radcliffe Cookes, in one of the oldest and loveliest country houses in England, Hellens Manor, between Ledbury and Ross-on-Wye. Hellens boasts a music room, a minstrel gallery and a stone hall with a great fireplace bearing the Black Prince's crest; it is full of beautiful paintings and furnishings; outside there is walled knot garden, a seventeenth-century dovecote and acres of parkland. To be housekeeper there would have been beyond the wildest dreams of a Munsley blacksmith's daughter. And Hellens was as convenient as it was seemingly unattainable, close to Bromsgerrow where Harriet's daughter Emily was being brought up with the Hill family. Robert Duffield Radcliffe Cooke, Harriet's employer, had no obvious cricketing connections, but W.G., who had mixed with influential local gentry, could still have been the mystery person who organised the Hellens job for Harriet.

It was such a good job that it is hard to see why she eventually left it for Bristol, a town she didn't know, far away from her family and daughter, to serve in a doctor's crowded house in unattractive Stapleton Road. And how did she hear about the new post? The move has no obvious motivation. If, however, Harriet had known W.G. well beforehand and in such a way that she would relish the pleasure of his further company, the whole thing becomes understandable.

At the same time, it also arouses other issues. The strain her presence would have put upon the household, for example, would have been considerable, even if Agnes and her Aunt Caroline were unaware of the existence of Harriet's children. There are two extant photographs of nearly fifty members of the Grace family in front of a haystack when out on a summer's nutting expedition at the village of Yate, near Chipping Sodbury, in 1891.* One or two servants have been recently identified among them, including both Harriet, then in her mid-forties, and her attractive daughter Emily. If the identifications are correct, it would certainly put Harriet and Emily into a particularly special position within the Grace household.

---

*   The party would have been hosted by Dr Alfred Grace and his wife. Their delightful seventeenth-century home in Chipping Sodbury (known then as View House) is now the Moda House Hotel.

It is tempting to see a symbolic triangle in the positions before the camera of W.G., Agnes and Harriet. In one of the photographs, too, Harriet has somewhat ostentatiously turned her face away from W.G. and Agnes (but, there again, she may have just been proudly showing off her profile).

The reasons for Harriet's return to Munsley are equally uncertain. Though Ashley Grange was hardly as grand as Hellens Manor, the change when she left the Graces' service was still a severe one. She returned to a tiny Munsley cottage, shared with a sister, with whom she sold groceries. It has to be possible, therefore, that sparks had recently flown at revelations within the Grace household and Agnes and Aunt Caroline had made it clear that, whether they stayed at Ashley Grange or moved to London, they were going to need to hire a new cook. In a more extreme scenario, Agnes and Aunt Caroline were even the ones who embraced the Crystal Palace proposition and, outraged by revelations concerning Harriet and Emily, insisted on the move to London.

14

A Lucrative Diversion

Crystal Palace and London County, 1899–1908

The new home, St Andrew's, 7 Lawrie Park Road, was a ten-minute walk away from Crystal Palace Park Road and the Sydenham entrance to the cricket ground. It was even closer in the opposite direction to Sydenham Station, then part of the London, Brighton and South Coast Railway. Walking down Lawrie Park Road from the station, we stop at the third turning on our left, Cricketers' Walk, where Laing Homes have put up a plaque in striking claret on a bright, four-storey block of flats, telling us that 'W.G. Grace, cricketer, lived in a house on this site'. It might have added the wistful rider, 'And had you come here in 1963, you could have seen Billy Griffith, M.C.C.'s secretary, unveiling a plaque on the original house'. The 1960s were dangerous times for historic houses. One moment W.G.'s old home was being celebrated with an L.C.C. blue plaque; the next, it was being knocked down to make way for Grace Lodge, a hostel for a bank, which, in its turn, was replaced by the block of flats. Many of the other houses in long, straight Lawrie Park Road have been luckier than St Andrew's, escaping the developers' bulldozers, and the next one down gives us a helpful idea of St Andrew's, though we have to imagine the yellow and red brickwork and terracotta plaques with their attractive floral designs before they were whitewashed.

Built in the 1880s, St Andrew's had none of the character or spaciousness of Ashley Grange but nevertheless offered the Graces more than enough good-sized rooms for their needs. Of their four children, only twenty-year-old Bessie and sixteen-year-old Charles moved with them to Sydenham, Charles leaving Clifton College for an engineering course within the Crystal Palace complex. Bertie, having finished at Cambridge, was now teaching at Oundle and Edgar was in the Royal Navy. Whenever Edgar was away, however, over the next few years, his wife Alice would stay at St Andrew's with their children. There was also Aunt Caroline, rising eighty but still providing Agnes with company in W.G.'s many absences. There were rooms, too, for three domestic servants. And the new cook.

For Agnes the return to London meant a closer relationship with her own branch of the family. Her mother had recently died and her unpredictable father, William Day, now in his mid-seventies, was currently sharing a smart address in the West End with Agnes' unmarried sister and two young ladies, one a singer, the other of private means. He still called himself a lithographer and publisher, but those times were long over.

The Graces had hardly moved into Lawrie Park Road when Bessie contracted typhoid. A two-month struggle ensued, but there could only be one outcome and in February 1899 she died. A tall, arresting girl with grey-green eyes, who had enjoyed a close rapport with her parents and inherited her father's athleticism, she had earlier proved an outstanding batsman, playing with real aplomb for the Ladies of Clifton. Her solitary grave at nearby Elmers End became a regular place of pilgrimage for her grieving parents.

Ironically, W.G.'s medical career had just ended, with a useful annuity, after a serious falling-out with the Bristol medical authorities over administrative rearrangements. He felt no financial need to carry on working as a doctor in London and would be busy, running both London County and Gloucestershire.

The first summer in Sydenham proved an extremely unsettling time. In early June 1899, not long before his fifty-first birthday, W.G. experienced mixed fortunes captaining England at Trent Bridge in the First Test against Australia. He removed Clem Hill with a brilliant one-handed catch at point off a searing cut, but also missed a chance he would have taken with ease in earlier, less bulky times. He bowled very economically, but did not take any wickets. In his first innings he scored 28 in an opening stand of 75 with Charles Fry, but his slowness between the wickets was painful. 'We lost innumerable singles on the off-side,' wrote Fry later, 'and I never dared call W.G. for a second run to the long-field.' When he was out for 1 in the second innings, his stumps spread-eagled, he was shocked to be jeered by the crowd. He planned to persevere, but on the advice of Fry and Ranjitsinhji he reluctantly stood down from the next Test in favour of Archie MacLaren. He would play no more international cricket.

Only days later came a further painful break with the past. Having opted out of Gloucestershire's first home fixture of 1899, he captained the county at Blackheath, The Oval, Hove and Lord's, but then took outraged exception to the committee's very reasonable request for a clear response on his availability for their season's remaining fixtures, and, still disorientated by the move to London and the tragic loss of Bessie, he penned a letter of resignation from Lawrie Park Road that ended with the much-quoted words, 'I have the greatest affection for the county of my birth, but for the committee, as a body, the greatest contempt'. Friends on the committee, like Arthur Bush and Walter Troup, attempted over late night drinks to effect a reconciliation, but he laughed the idea off. The break was all the more bitter in that E.M. was still the county secretary.

The crises of 1899 were reflected in his bare thirteen first-class matches and his average of only 23 with no centuries, but in captaining the Gentlemen against the Players he scored 60 at The Oval and 78 at Lord's and, as the new supremo at Crystal Palace, averaged 84 in his twenty minor matches, with centuries against Beckenham, Croydon, Ealing, Sydenham and Worcestershire (175 not out at Worcester). There was major disappointment, however, when London County's application to join the county championship in 1900 was rejected, though it was given first-class status for games with individual counties and touring teams.

* * *

Lord's has three particularly fascinating illustrations of W.G.'s years at Crystal Palace. We find in the museum both his London County cap and boots from that period. Just as Lord Sheffield had used the M.C.C. colours and added purple, so for his new cap W.G. combined stripes of yellow and red with green. Somewhat bizarrely, just one of a pair of large white boots is displayed. Made of thick skin with calf linings, his boots would have been thought extremely modern in 1900, for ones of similar style were still being used sixty years later.*

Both boots and the cap reappear in a bronze statue of W.G. that adorns the Coronation Garden. It is the work of the Dutch-born Australian sculptor Louis Laumen, produced by the Melbourne firm Fundere as part of a 'speculative initiative producing life-size (or bigger) images of sporting and historical figures' and shipped to England in 1999. It was on show at Nevil Road, but M.C.C. leapt in and clinched a deal. The statue was inspired by the only surviving film of W.G. in action, batting in the nets at Hastings in 1901. As we sit in the Coronation Garden, watching the larger-than-life W.G. turning the ball off his legs, head well over it, eyes fiercely focused, left elbow suitably bent, we can observe the strong technique that enabled a fifty-one-year-old to score five centuries for his new club in 1899. It took the sculptor five hundred hours of work. There were eight weeks of preparation, followed by another eight weeks of the sculpting process – 'packing and splashing' clay onto a skeleton made of steel rods and tubing. 'You don't go crazy and hope something emerges,' commented Laumen. 'I work the clay for six to eight weeks, for hours a day, every day, feeling and searching for the person through movement and balance.'

W.G.'s initial performances for London County were extremely creditable. He was eleventh in the national averages in 1900 at over 42 for his 1,277 first-class runs. He scored even more in his many club matches, averaging over 53. In 1902 the magazine *Cricket* loyally stated, 'Even now, at the advanced age of fifty-four, he is worth his place in almost any team in the world'. But then, in the wet season of 1903, he began to struggle. There was still one big highlight that year, however, when Gloucestershire, with whom reconciliation had at last been effected, came in early June to Crystal Palace.

* * *

---

*   Exhibitions are constantly reorganised. Shortly after the book was written, W.G.'s London County cap (presented to M.C.C. in 1962) was moved from public display to the Committe Room.

We can approach the ground today from the same Sydenham entrance that he used for London County's match with Gloucestershire that summer in 1903. Having greeted the gate-keeper, he strode briskly along a curving path that straightens out beside a huge expanse of playing field, and started a majestic progress towards his distant pavilion with acolytes trailing in his wake. He soon passed, on his right, the beautifully kept bowling greens of the other club he created and managed. He himself regularly played bowls for London County and only that year had founded the English Bowls Association. In 1903, too, as the arranger of the first international competitions, he led England against Scotland at Crystal Palace, the first of several such occasions.

As we follow the same path today, the only landmark to help us is a modern pagoda, housing a bell commemorating the First World War. It faces out onto flat and strangely disused playing fields, the amorphous site of W.G.'s eight-acre, six-sided cricket ground. A Crystal Palace Cricket Club, swiftly subsumed by London County, had been functioning here for several years, centred around a small pavilion that W.G. used for storage. Although the square and outfield were of decent quality, W.G. had insisted on both being upgraded to the very highest level, ensuring that he would be operating on one of the best batting surfaces in the country.

As we look out from the pagoda, the wicket (which ran more or less parallel with the far line of trees and, behind them, Crystal Palace Park Road) was a little to the right. We are viewing the nearer set of stumps from the position of wide third-man to a right-hander; the further set, from somewhere between deep-mid-wicket and long-on.

We carry along the path and where it curves left, just before the children's play area, we reach the unmarked site of W.G.'s pavilion. It was set at an angle from the path, in a corner position facing out towards the pitch. It was here, in June 1903, that he signalled his arrival for the Gloucestershire match in his usual way, with a shrill blast of a whistle, and was quickly surrounded by eager helpers, awaiting orders. Bill Murch, the former Gloucestershire bowler whom W.G. had brought with him to act as sergeant-major to the ground staff, responded somewhat tardily, partly because he had just been told he was making up numbers for the depleted Gloucestershire team and partly because he was becoming increasingly deaf. 'Murch, you're sacked!' cried W.G. 'Don't worry,' muttered Murch to a worried-looking friend, 'I get sacked about twice a day.' For all W.G.'s aggressive bluster, an air of cheerful friendliness pervaded the pavilion. Soon Ernest Dyer, the chief pavilion attendant, whom W.G. had also brought from Bristol, was hovering in the home dressing-room, W.G.'s favourite pads at the ready, for his chief job was to attend to every aspect of W.G.'s cricket gear.

The two-storey pavilion that the Crystal Palace Company specially erected for W.G. at a cost over £3,000 was the hub of his ground. Built in red brick with weather boarding and wooden railings, it could seat five hundred members and friends. There were dressing-rooms, store-rooms and a spectators' gallery on the first floor, with two dining-rooms below as well as a servery, bar, offices, and a retiring room for ladies. In the basement, at the rear, was the all-important beer cellar. Radiators that supplied the whole building were connected to a basement boiler. It was well sheltered by the trees on the slope behind it, that leads up to the next level of the Crystal Palace gardens, where, today, the end of a vast National Sports Centre building is almost, but not quite, directly above. The pavilion was, likewise, conveniently near the tree-lined Grand Central Walk that took visitors up to the gleaming Crystal Palace, where members of London County enjoyed free entrance and rooms reserved exclusively for them.

W.G. regularly took a net before play began. The London County ground bowlers had already climbed up the path beside the pavilion to the nets that were situated inside an athletics track within a cycle track (in the area occupied today by the N.S.C. complex). With the Crystal Palace itself in the background and a classical rotondo in the middle distance, it was a fascinating place in which to practise.

After the four-year stand-off with Gloucestershire, W.G. naturally viewed the fixture with enthusiasm. On the first day of the match his old county made 397, Harry Wrathall's 160 including one fine on-drive for six off W.G. that ended up in the road outside. For Wrathall it was wonderful recompense for an occasion at Lord's when W.G. had accused him of laziness and consigned him, over after over, to long-off. But despite the high total, W.G., who had given himself a generous number of overs, felt content enough with his figures of 6-104.

London County were 20-2 when W.G. went out at the start of the second day's play with Richard Brooks, a thirty-nine-year-old solicitor. He enjoyed an early let-off, having hoisted a leg-break from Ted Spry high to the mid-wicket boundary (somewhere near the pagoda) where fair-haired William Penfold, one of London County's ground bowlers and a part-time bricklayer, subbing for Gloucestershire, dropped the catch. Penfold was later presented by a grateful W.G.with a cricket ball signed by members of the 1902 Australian touring team. To have made a duck against Gloucestershire would have been deeply mortifying. Even with W.G. enjoying the reprieve, at 25-4 things looked bad. But W.G. featured in strong stands with Les Poidevin, an Australian medical student who later qualified for Lancashire, and the twenty-year-old future captain of Essex and England, Johnnie Douglas, and was his old relentless self as he went on to 150 (in 215 minutes) before Spry caught him at cover-point off his own bowling. 'There were several dangerous strokes,' commented one reporter, 'but his placing to leg was as well-timed as ever.' The on-side was his favoured area throughout. As regards mobility, one witness reckoned that 'between the wickets he was not so slow as on some former occasions', but then he had a point to prove with Gloucestershire, an extra incentive for effort.

It had been a remarkable achievement for a fifty-four-year-old, but, disappointingly, there were less than five hundred spectators and they looked lost in the capacious ground ringed with tiered seating. Next to the pavilion there was a long, roofed stand, with its back to the Grand Central Walk, capable of holding 1,500 people (to be charged five shillings each) but largely empty. Some years earlier, news that Grace was batting would have been the signal for a mass withdrawal of labour from nearby factories and offices. But the London County matches were thought merely show events, unrelated to the serious business of the county championship.

The home team, by necessity, was a mixture of promising youngsters, good club players and foreigners.* Gloucestershire, one of the poorer counties that season, had not put out their strongest eleven. Their four main bowlers were all young professionals at the very start of their careers, including twenty-year-old left-arm spinner Charlie Parker, making his debut. Though the regular wicket-keeper Jack Board was in the team, the gloves were entrusted to a young unknown, Arthur Nott, and when Nott was allowed to bowl four expensive overs, his incompetent deputy let through 23 byes. The county's regular captain Walter Troup wasn't playing, and his deputy, Gilbert Jessop, was 'absent injured' for two of the days. When Gloucestershire's ten men lost the match by being bowled out for 61, there were rumours of their desire to catch an early train back to Bristol. It was hardly the kind of atmosphere that was going to attract a large public.

* * *

London County's regular return fixtures with Cambridge University, Derbyshire, Leicestershire, M.C.C., Surrey and Warwickshire, with occasional appearances from touring elevens from Australia, South Africa and the West Indies, were not enough to establish Crystal Palace as a serious cricket centre. Lord Harris' Kent and Lord Hawke's Yorkshire were notable in keeping their distance. So, too, Middlesex, Notts, Essex and Hampshire. The counties' lack of enthusiasm for a London intruder was understandable. The current structure of English cricket had taken many years to achieve a position of dominance. The urge to maintain the status quo was strong.

London County's first-class status ceased after 1904. For four more seasons there was just club cricket with only the odd first-class fixture played by the 'Gentlemen of England' and 'Mr W.G. Grace's Eleven'. Even so, W.G. was not best pleased when his employers, the Crystal Palace Company, finally ended his contract. They were to go bankrupt the next year.

The ground was converted to public tennis courts in the 1920s, later replaced by a couple of football pitches. By 1960, W.G.'s pavilion was in a forlorn state of decay and demolished. Kent County Cricket Club showed interest for a few years in the 1990s. A small square was re-laid on which the Club and Ground side entertained Indian Under 19 touring teams that included Tendulkar, Dravid,

---

* The side facing Gloucestershire included two other Australians in addition to Poidevin: the veteran Test player Billy Murdoch and fast bowler Alex Kermode. There were also a young New Zealander, Dan Reese, and an outstandingly good fast bowler from Holland, Carst Postuma.

Ganguly and Jadeja. Today it is a paradise for jogging, dog-walking and cheerful gossip, yet to see this historic and attractive site without any cricket on a glorious Saturday afternoon in the height of the summer is to feel a sense of loss.

Perhaps it is the fault of W.G.'s legacy. London County had proved a delightful and remunerative retirement package for him, but his generous backers had hoped for something rather more. There were occasional big matches with sizeable crowds, but, overall, W.G. seemed more interested in providing the best of entertainment for his friends than worrying whether the tiered benches were filling up satisfactorily. The last-surviving London County cricketer, James Gilman, interviewed in his old age, tellingly picked out the catering as 'The Old Man's' major concern. He remembered the lunches in the pavilion as 'sumptuous, with hock and claret on the table' and W.G. not stinting himself: 'He had a real whack of the roast, followed by a big lump of cheese. He also tackled his whisky and selzer, which was always his drink'.

* * *

Amid the Edwardian feasting and fun there was also much sadness. W.G.'s sisters Annie and Fanny both died in Bristol soon after his move away. Then, in 1905, six years after the death of Bessie, Bertie died from complications after appendicitis at the age of thirty.

W.G. Grace junior had struggled gallantly to live up to his name. Though he was not blessed with his father's fine eyesight, he was tall and strong enough to attain many sporting successes, dwarfed though they always were by his father's achievements and spoilt by his expectations. He had fulfilled his father's hopes by captaining the Clifton eleven and winning his Blue. But his successes were never enough. His father wanted more. When in 1894 Cambridge failed to include him for an early-season fixture with M.C.C., W.G. picked him instead for M.C.C. and they duly opened the innings together at Fenner's. Grace junior made a duck, Grace senior 139. In the return match at Lord's exactly the same thing happened. Grace junior failed and Grace senior made 196. Though Bertie did well in his first Varsity Match, he will go down in cricket history for scoring a pair the next year, while his crestfallen father looked on aghast and Agnes and Bessie wept in the stands. W.G., with the best of intentions, kept blundering insensitively into his son's life. He insisted on coming up to play at Oundle and scored 141, while poor Bertie failed. Nobody noticed, a week later, when Bertie himself, playing for Oundle Town, scored 141. He was a sensitive and scholarly man, his withdrawn and unemotional character making him something of an oddity in the family, but he dutifully turned out for London County in the school holidays of 1901-03. He had managed an average of 15 in his fifty-seven first-class matches and had taken 42 fairly expensive wickets, before moving to the Isle of Wight, a little further away from his suffocating father, to teach at the Royal Naval College, Osborne. And there he died. He was buried with Bessie at Elmers End.

Bertie's death prefaced a series of cricketing valedictions. In 1906, around his fifty-eighth birthday, W.G. played the last of his eighty-five games for the Gentlemen, scoring 74 at The Oval. In April 1908, in his sixtieth year, 'the huge man with the iron-grey beard' appeared in his last first-class match, captaining a Gentlemen of England eleven against Surrey at The Oval and scoring forty runs, 'his driving and pulling' being 'an object lesson to many a young player'. That August, he made his last two appearances at Lord's, playing for London County against M.C.C. and for M.C.C. against Dorsetshire. He scored 33 in his final Lord's innings.

15

A Rural Finale

The Mottingham years, 1909–15

The blue plaque on St Andrew's, which so briefly had told passers-by in Sydenham that W.G. had once lived there, was rescued from the bulldozers and soon afterwards repositioned over the front door of a house six miles away in Kent. On a sunny day in July 1966, Stuart Chiesman, the chairman of Kent County Cricket Club, gave the plaque its second unveiling at a ceremony and celebratory fête attended by G. Neville Weston, the leading authority on W.G., and Neville Sugden, the cricketing vicar who helped instigate the project. The plaque's new home was Fairmount in Mottingham, south of Eltham.

* * *

The Graces moved to Fairmount in July 1909. It is unclear whether or not a return to Bristol was considered and why in the end they chose Kent, but there were several obvious attractions. After suburban Sydenham, the village of Mottingham, surrounded by farms and fields that escaped the developers until the 1920s, offered W.G. the outdoor country life he so loved; they were still not far from Bessie and Bertie's grave at Elmers End; and the South Eastern Railways provided an admirable train service from Mottingham–Eltham railway station, just a quarter-of-an-hour's walk away, connecting easily to London and also to the Royal Naval dockyards, where twenty-nine-year-old Charles, still living at home, was working as an electrical engineer. There is the possibility, too, that they were helped in their choice by the Kent connections of Agnes' maternal aunt, Marian Coleman, who at nearly eighty came to live with them, good company for Agnes' paternal aunt Caroline, who had now been part of the Grace household for nearly thirty years and was approaching ninety.

From Agnes' point of view, the new home, with its ample hallway, twelve large rooms, high ceilings, attractive mouldings and leaded lights, offered the same kind of comfortable and spacious accommodation as St. Andrew's. It was always important that her Gilbert had plenty of space.

* * *

The Fairmount Care Home has grown a little since W.G.'s day to accommodate more residents, its projecting right-hand wing acquiring a couple of extra floors. The façade, too, had a gentler atmosphere in Edwardian times with its covering of ivy. Instead of the asphalt parking area in front of the yellow-brick house we must imagine a lawn full of circular flowerbeds, around which a narrow driveway curved to the front door from the two entrances in Mottingham Lane.

Fairmount was aptly named. In the era immediately before the First World War it still stood well apart from Mottingham village, on the top of a small but steep hill to its immediate west, and enjoyed extensive views over the countryside along with half-a-dozen other villas of the 1870s, each set in an acre or more of land. The Graces' neighbours were all well-to-do. Sir George Woodward of The Grange, for example, was a Knight and Alderman of the City of London. His gardener and family lived at Grange Lodge, his coachman and family at Grange Stables. There were several other lodges and 'motor houses' for chauffeurs and their families. The Graces, by contrast, lived comparatively simply in their rented home, relying on pony-and-trap rather than motor cars and limiting themselves to only three live-in servants – a cook, a ladies' maid (for the two elderly aunts) and parlourmaid.

From the beginning W.G. spent many hours in his huge garden – it was said to have stretched back half a mile – employing a number of helpers who were placed under the care of Dyer, his former personal attendant at the Crystal Palace pavilion. An attractive sunken garden was created at the far end with a large ornamental fishpond. In due course, too, W.G. would develop a most productive area for vegetables – his asparagus bed was said to be particularly impressive – and other interesting features included a chicken run, a clock-golf course and a cricket net.

A Mottingham resident, reminiscing in the 1940s, mentioned regular visits to Fairmount: 'Once a week W.G. practised in the nets - he had his own nets in the back garden. And one night a week I went to bowl to him for half-an-hour. If I bowled a bad ball, he would tell me in plain words what he thought of me...' Other memories included 'the broad shoulders, the long beard and the happy face'. W.G. was well liked in the village, and, when playing cricket, 'always had the happiest face of all'. Quite what the other residents on the hill made of the cricket net, or, for that matter, the chickens, is not clear, but certainly in the eyes of the villagers, if not necessarily the knights and aldermen, the Graces counted as gentry, deservedly enjoying on Sundays one of the best pews in St Andrew's Church.

* * *

There had been no cricket at Sydenham in the year of the move, the gates of the London County club being firmly shut, and by the time they had settled at Fairmount the season was over. So it was with much relish that W.G., with Charles alongside, joined Eltham Cricket Club in 1910. Founded back in the 1860s, Eltham was considered one of the best clubs in Kent, and though it plays today in

New Eltham, a considerable distance away from Fairmount, its Edwardian home was conveniently nearby, within walking distance.

We can follow father and son as they go there. In a matter of minutes, they have descended the hill and entered the village, passing by three regular ports-of-call, The Porcupine (an inn rebuilt in the 1920s), Jobbin's, a bakery with pretty striped awnings, and William Turner's coal office (both long since gone), before turning left down a narrow country lane, today's Court Road. This led them past fields and the little church of St Andrew's, built not many years before their arrival.

We must briefly pause at St Andrew's, for it was important to W.G. in his last years. Indeed, the Graces were involved in its programme of building development during which Aunt Caroline paid for an entrance porch of mock-Tudor. W.G., a little more conservatively, decreed that after his death the church's new vestry should have the Pembroke Table that had served him well as a working-desk. Complete with a commemorative plaque, 'the former parishioner's gift' is still much cherished.

It was in this church, in 1911, that he paused in silence to contemplate life without Teddy. Bad news had kept coming from Thornbury. First, of a stroke and paralysis – and it was so hard to think of the passionate Teddy suddenly immobile and speechless; then of his death. They had all gone to the funeral at Christ Church. W.G. had been very moved by the roads lined with respectful villagers as the coffin was brought from Thornbury in a slow, twelve-mile cortège. Dear Teddy had been doctoring to the end, just as he'd kept up his hunting and cricket, scorning the onset of arthritis. Nothing would stop that brother of his! He had enjoyed a good life. Four wives. Seventeen children. Not all had made it to adulthood, and the very first had been sadly handicapped. But Teddy had pressed on through it all, the squire of Thornbury, lording it over everyone from that lovely home of his, Park House. What energy! He had never missed a dance – he was nimble in the ballroom – or an opportunity for rough shooting. For nearly forty years he'd been the county's secretary, just as their father had wished it, keeping going almost to the end. They hadn't unfortunately seen eye to eye with much regularity over the years, but it was thrilling to hear from John Dann that a marvellous memorial for Teddy was planned, a rose window in the new chancel that was being added on to Christ Church. Teddy would have loved that. So, too, the tablet in the Thornbury church where he'd rarely missed a Sunday evening service.

W.G. and Charles have pushed on ahead, cutting across a field to their right, a brisk walk taking them in five minutes or so to Chapel Farm, a picturesque old farmhouse, close by a duck pond, with windows that rattled eerily on windless days and barns full of old haywains and leather harnesses that would have delighted John Constable. The cricket ground was just beyond, the other side of the farm. In contrast to dilapidated Chapel Farm it was beautifully looked after, with clusters of fine old trees protecting it from the wind, and a wooden pavilion distinctly above the standards of the day.

We can't follow W.G. along the path across the fields, for it has all been built over. Instead we return down Court Road, turn left at the A208 and take the second left, Chapel Farm Road, which brings us to the Coldharbour Leisure Centre. One part of W.G.'s old ground lies under these modern playing fields – the area directly in front of the netball and tennis courts. The other part, however, has now disappeared under the houses of Altash and Witherston Ways.

W.G. played his first match here on 28 May 1910, getting an irritating early lbw decision against Granville, a club from nearby Lee,* but he was soon making 30 at Blackheath and 71 against Charlton Park. In his seventeen matches that season he averaged nearly 28. In 1911-13 he scored nearly 800 runs for an average of 20. He enjoyed himself immensely in these late years and was always the fun-loving master of ceremonies, making each and every game a memorable one for all participants. In the field he was no longer really a contributor, but his Eltham team-mates devotedly ran around for him, and he repaid their generosity at the end of each season by gathering an eleven of his own to play the club in a concluding fixture of supreme conviviality.

In 1914 he managed to fit in eighteen matches before the outbreak of the First World War ended the season abruptly, able to average around 25 at the age of sixty-six. The pitches, of course, were distinctly more sporting than the featherbeds at the Crystal Palace, and in one home game he was struck above the eye by a ball that lifted unexpectedly. For someone who had batted against the best fast bowlers in the land back on the treacherous surfaces of the 1860s and early 1870s, it was nothing to make a fuss about.

* * *

His final innings of all was played for Eltham on 25 July 1914 in an away fixture at nearby Grove Park. Their home ground at the time was by the Durham dairy farm off Marvels Lane, quite close to the river Quaggy, a site now occupied by the City of London School Sports Field. On a visit on a bright summer's day we find a helpful head groundsman. Yes, he believed that W.G. had played here. That was certainly the legend. Over on the Grove Park Road side of the ground, perhaps where the 1st eleven now play, beyond the large, multi-purpose pavilion. The wicket was most probably sited between the pavilion and square.

In 1914 the Grove Park pavilion was the usual simple wooden construction with a couple of communal changing-rooms and a bar. The ground was small and tree-lined, very different from the flat, open expanses of the school's sports field. Amid the cheery socialising that preceded the toss, a proliferation of brightly striped blazers added a bold dash of colour to the scene. W.G. himself favoured his old London County blazer that had done good service since his move to

---

* W.G. seems to have presided over all the local grounds, including Lee, to judge by a story that he was approached about the borrowing of the Lee ground. 'You can borrow the lot: ground, gear, waitresses and all,' he replied. Then his eyes glinted. 'But mind you, all the crockery you smash you'll have to pay for!'

London. The whole gathering centred around him, and he seemed to find time for a few jocular words with everyone, from Edward Tyler, the Master of the local Workhouse, to Cyril Luffman, son of the vicar of St Augustine's. He preferred to bat low in the order in these late games, but this time, as he entered the team in the scorebook, he put himself in sixth. Charles opened the innings but was one of the four wickets to fall when, at 31-4, W.G. appeared. It was a theatrical entrance. There was first a certain amount of prodding of the pitch delivered with a fierce look of reproof. Then the elaborate taking of his guard and a long, careful survey of the fielders' positions. Finally, dwarfing the stumps, he faced down the wicket with the usual look of bland ferocity, left foot inclined towards the bowler, a mesmerising figure, ready to take advantage of any faintheartedness in his opponent. He was soon off the mark, with a drive that allowed a slowly taken single. (He had brusquely turned down the Grove Park offer of a runner.) Further wickets fell, but his concentration was unwavering. With Eltham's young David Henshall he added 71 for the 7th wicket in an hour and twenty minutes. At the tea-time declaration, he was 69 not out. 'He got his runs all round the wicket,' recalled one of the umpires later in the *Memorial Biography*, 'being especially strong on the offside.' Several of his six fours came from well-timed square and late cuts off the fastest bowler. If he had accepted the offer of a runner, he would have added yet another century to his long list.*

It was to be the final practical example of a batting technique that has challenged adequate summary over the years. C.B. Fry's famous comment (when ghosting for Ranji) that 'he made utility the criterion of style' still remains the most penetrating and was later helpfully enlarged upon by biographer Eric Midwinter:

> He concentrated on playing every shot rather than specialising... He was not aridly mechanical, but extremely functional. This was in the Victorian tradition, but he eschewed what was often its matching trait, that of fussy ornateness. Grace had all the efficiency but none of the over-decorative fidgetiness of the typical item of the Great Exhibition. His batting manner was sparse, strong and clean as Gregorian plain-chant, and it was highly attractive for that reason.

He turned out in one further match, at Chapel Farm on 8 August, but didn't bat. Fifteen days later the First World War began, ending the season. He did not play again.There were occasional sightings of him in 1915. On Whit Monday he turned up at Catford where he had agreed to appear in a star-studded match for war charities, but in the end felt not well enough to do so, taking around a collecting box instead. In August he went out with Agnes to watch the Lewisham Scout Troop's sports day, held at Mottingham. It was his last remembered public appearance.

---

*   The bat used in this last innings, a Gunn and Moore, survives in a private collection.

On 9 October W.G. was taken ill while working in the garden and helped inside the house by the faithful Dyer. He had suffered a small stroke but his speech was unimpaired and he still had the use of his limbs. Three days later Agnes explained his condition to Frederick Ashley-Cooper, preparing a book on E.M.

> The doctor is ill & may not do anything in the way of going through your proofs for a week at least from now – he was taken ill on Saturday but read the first lot of proofs through & told me a lot of mistakes but they are not marked, & I am sure that I could not remember all, he would be very sorry for it to be published with such a number of errors. If you must have the proofs back before he can revise them, I must send them to you, but I am not allowed to bother him in any way.

His condition worsened soon afterwards and he died at Fairmount on the morning of 23 October.

* * *

He had told Agnes he wished to be buried with Bessie and Bertie, the daughter with whom he had much in common and the son he had struggled to understand. Burial in Beckenham meant one final break with his Bristol past. Only three months earlier, Agnes had accompanied him on his last visit to Downend, for the funeral at Christ Church of John Dann, whose last resting-place, in a prominent position by the West Door, was marked with a fine Celtic cross, recently restored by his descendants.[*] Six of W.G.'s brothers and sisters were now buried at Christ Church, as well as his parents, Uncle Alfred and a host of other relatives. It was a church he knew better, and loved more, than any other. But to leave Bessie and Bertie alone was unthinkable.

Opened in the 1880s alongside the South Norwood Country Park, the cemetery at Elmers End of over forty acres was pleasantly landscaped with maturing trees and shrubs. Today's crematorium was originally one of two mortuary chapels, balancing each other either side of the main avenue. Unfortunately the chapel on the right, used for W.G.'s service, was bombed in the Second World War and later pulled down, but its overgrown site is still clearly visible.

Sir Home Gordon's description in the *Memorial Biography* gives an eye-witness account:

> It was on a bitterly cold afternoon, October 26, 1915, that a great gathering assembled at Elmer's End Cemetery to pay the last tribute of respect . . . The

---

[*] The Pigeons. Bob Pigeon, John and Blanche Dann's great-grandson, points out that the family's medical control of the area was further strengthened by the Grace–Pigeon intermarriage that began when the eldest of the Danns' daughters married Dr John Pigeon in 1893.

church was filled to overflowing and, at the conclusion of the first portion of the service, the lengthy procession of mourners made its way to the grave, where, under the shadow of a hawthorn tree, the hero of cricket was laid to rest beside a son and daughter who had preceded him into the land of shadows.

If we go to the far side of the overgrown site of the chapel, we can follow the path the mourners took (in the direction of Birkbeck railway station). The Graces' grave with its simple marble cross is comparatively easy to spot as it is meticulously looked after (by the Forty Club) and shines a bright white amongst its grey, heavily-weathered companions. The coffin was born on the shoulders of eight bare-headed pallbearers, all wearing long black overcoats in the freezing weather. Charles, who was serving as a Captain in the Fortress Engineers, followed immediately behind the coffin, accompanying his mother, cap in hand with a black armband on his army greatcoat. Edgar was absent, for he was serving with the Royal Navy in the Dardanelles.

Khaki was much in evidence among the black. Large numbers from two generations of cricket's golden age, both amateur and professional, had somehow managed to come to pay their respects, with Ranjitsinhji in uniform attracting particular attention. Lord Harris was another noted celebrity, a fellow tourist, years previously, in North America. Survivors from the trips to Australia included Frizzy Bush and Goldney Radcliffe. All looked tired and dazed. Tears flowed openly. Could there really be an end to so much zest for life, so much outrageous fun, such scorn for boring conformity?

For each of the mourners there were certain special memories of their own. For Harry Preston, a Brighton hotel owner and boxing impresario, it was the boyish sense of fun that stayed uppermost in the mind. He remembered the time twelve years ago when W.G. had come down to Bournemouth to play for the Gentlemen of the South at the end-of-season festival. On one late evening at the Grand Hotel, a whole group of them were nattering away over tumblers of whisky when, and at around 1.00 in the morning there came from W.G. a piercing roar: 'Wouldn't it be rather a lark if we all raced up the stairs to the top of the hotel and down again, and the last man stood drinks all round?' Away they all tore. Down they all came, with W.G. obstructing those who sought to pass him. The last man paid up. They drank his health. And off they went again, to the very top of the stairs and down, W.G. again successfully fighting off his rivals at the tail of the field. They'd have done it again – it was such terrific fun – but for the sudden appearance of anxious faces, querying whether the hotel was suffering some terrible catastrophe . . .

A.A. Thomson tells of another mourner, a serving soldier who had just arrived home on leave from the Western Front and felt impelled to go along. He lingered on after the vast throng had 'melted away into the cold, autumnal twilight', and, as 'an old-fashioned schoolmasterly type brought up on the Victorian poets', he began to think of 'the slow, melancholy music' of Tennyson's 'Morte d'Arthur' with Sir Bedivere sadly watching the death of the great King:

> This day unsolders all the goodliest fellowship
> Whereof this world holds record...

The poem refused to go away as he mused on the loss of W.G.:

> He thought of the vaguely noble figure of King Arthur, the misty shadow of a poet's dream; and he thought of the wholly different 'king' who lay there in the still open grave but a few yards away, who had been so robust, so earthy, so richly endowed, not poetically, but in flesh and blood, in his own 'big assemblance', with the spirit of English laughter and the summer country scene...

Thomson, writing in the security and optimism of the 1950s, concludes his biography with a wonderfully emotional final paragraph:

> The leaves of the three nearby trees had nearly all gone, but in the gathering dusk a light wind swayed their branches. On the wind there came to his imagination a whisper, faint but growing, and somehow it seemed that in the whisper was a promise – a promise that 'the goodliest fellowship' would never finally be unsoldered, and that, despite war and winter, summer's world of happy days would come again, would always come again... He walked down the curved path into the broad walk towards the gate. It was almost dark. The wind was still blowing and in the sound of it the end-line of the poem swelled like a trumpet-call:
>
> > And the new sun rose, bringing the new year.

16

A Homeward Journey

From The Graces to Lord's

The Roman poet Horace might not have played much cricket, but he certainly understood the transitory nature of things. *Eheu fugaces*, he wrote, *labuntur anni*. 'Alas! The years slip by and flee away!' We have been depending on our imaginations all trip because we, too, are troubled by the *anni fugaces*, and even now, when we are visiting a fairly modern pub on our penultimate stop, we are still having to imagine things as they were. The pub (or, rather, Bar and Grill) is called The Graces. It's on the corner of Elmers End Road and Witham Road, next door to Birkbeck Station and just the other side of the railway line from the cemetery and W.G.'s grave. When it opened in 1966, it was called the Dr W.G. Grace.

It introduces us to the Revd Neville Sugden, a former vicar in nearby Beckenham, whose services to W.G. include the Fairmount plaque, and without whom the grave at Elmers End would not be in the fine condition it is today. It was Neville Sugden, too, who heard that Trumans were opening a pub by the cemetery, persuaded them to call it after W.G., insisted that it have a bar 22 yards long, organised a big opening party, pulled the first pint, blessed the house, and did his best to fill it with Grace memorabilia, including a magnificent mirror, 'tinged with copper with the head of Dr W.G. Grace superimposed'.

Fifty years on, we can still raise a glass in honour of Dr W.G. Grace in the same, unique pub. In 2014 it reopened (as The Graces) after an expensive extension and makeover of attractive modernity that has given it a splendidly airy new bar and dining room. All of the Revd Sugden's Grace mementoes have, alas, long since slipped by and fled away, but the current management, very aware of the pub's heritage and deeply interested in W.G., are currently having the old pub sign restored. Perhaps by our next visit it will be sited in a prime location. All lovers of cricket history, in the meantime, are urged to make their way to The Graces to toast W.G. and the Revd Sugden and to admire the new 22-yard bar.

A pleasant lunch at The Graces sparked further thoughts of 1915, Fairmount and Elmers End. Agnes stayed on at Fairmount for a while. Aunt Caroline eventually died there in 1917 at the age of ninety-seven, and was buried with her late husband back in Bristol at Christ Church. In due course Agnes moved away from Mottingham to Hawkhurst to be close to Charles, who had married and started a family. There, in 1930 at the age of seventy-six, she died. She was duly buried at Elmers End with Gilbert, Bertie and Bessie.*

The grave at Elmers End inevitably became a shrine for cricket lovers. In 1948, on the centenary of W.G.'s birth, it was visited by Don Bradman and other members of the Australian 'Invincibles' for a wreath-laying ceremony of remembrance. By the 1960s, however, when it was showing serious signs of neglect, Neville Sugden and a Dutch cricketer Ray Ingelse, both members of the Forty Club, formed a Memorial Fund with the aim of restoring the grave to a fitting condition for the fiftieth anniversary of W.G.'s death in October 1965.

Sugden, whose love of cricket was complemented by an excellent eye for a racehorse, was a determined character, who as a young man had kept wicket for the Oxford Authentics and fought with the British Expeditionary Force in the Second World War, being stretchered off from Dunkirk in 1940, the very last soldier to be evacuated. He was the right person to be acting as Hon. Treasurer of the Memorial Fund and when 23 October 1965 came round, there he was, standing by a wonderfully restored memorial and leading a graveside service at which a marble tablet was unveiled and a laurel wreath laid in M.C.C. colours. The lesson was read by the former England captain Arthur Gilligan, the President of the Forty Club.

Twenty-five years later, in 1990 on the 75th anniversary of W.G.'s death, another local vicar, the Revd Canon Derek Carpenter of St George's Church, Beckenham, led another wreath-laying ceremony at the grave. This followed a service in St George's the previous day, where Christopher Martin-Jenkins spoke movingly of W.G. and the Christian connotations of the word 'grace'. The Revd Neville Sugden was present on both occasions, for among the growing number of books in our back seat library is a slim booklet that he himself had privately printed to commemorate his ceremony of 1965, inscribed to Martin-Jenkins on the day of the St George's service.

Eight years later, in 1998 on the 150th anniversary of W.G.'s birth, the Revd Carpenter led a further graveside service. He also compiled, like his predecessor, a booklet for the occasion, including the Martin-Jenkins address of 1990. All the Graces and the Pococks, with their strong evangelical faith to which W.G. himself was happy enough to subscribe, would have said a loud 'amen' to its conclusion:

> By the grace of God there is the potential for grace in all of us, not, alas, in the sense of playing with gracefulness, or in such a way as to emulate W.G. himself, though perhaps those of us still active as players, just about, can at least try to play with good grace, but certainly, if we seek it, we all have a

---

*   Edgar, who became an admiral after a most distinguished career in the Royal Navy, died at Devonport in 1937, aged sixty-one. Charles collapsed and died in 1938, aged fifty-six, while batting near Bexhill-on-Sea for a club team he himself had started when managing director of the Weald Electricity Company. He had just scored a boundary.

potential for finding and conveying grace in the divine sense. It was surely the grace of God which gave us, which gave cricket, W.G. Grace, the doctor, the great cricketer.

* * *

The afternoon traffic is dense, as we begin the drive homewards. It was a good lunch at The Graces, and as we leave the Elmers End Road further and further behind, the reflection grows that the re-naming of the pub was, in fact, highly appropriate. The family of the Graces was all-important. W.G. was indebted to it and dependent on it all his life. It is surely right, therefore, for future pilgrims to Elmers End, when visiting the nearby hostelry which, as Neville Sugden wrote, is only 'a boundary throw from the grave', to raise a glass not just to the great cricketer, but also to Agnes, Martha, Dr Henry and the whole highly talented family.

One short, final stop remains, for we cannot conclude our journey without a salute to the Grace Gates at Lord's on the St John's Wood Road. Designed by Herbert Baker and opened by Stanley Jackson in 1923, they are both attractive and well positioned. Though their two gateways are somewhat narrow for modern transport needs, the M.C.C. membership quite rightly voted for them not to be moved, when, in 2006, that possibility arose. It is surely only fitting that W.G., who did so much for Lord's, should enjoy the most significant location.

Neville Cardus, whose *Days In The Sun* was published when the Grace Gates were brand-new, featured their site in a typically romantic piece in which, on a quiet and mellow June morning, he imagined a 'gleaming hansom cab at the entrance' and, of course, 'a black-bearded man, looking mountainous in everyday clothes' climbing down. No cricket lover at Lord's, Cardus explained, could keep the thought of Grace from his mind, 'for though Grace was a Gloucestershire man surely he larded the green earth at Lord's till the very spirit of him may be said to have gone into the grass'. 'The amplitude of Grace,' wrote Cardus, transcended 'Gloucestershire and his little day'.

The 'amplitude of Grace' was certainly awesome. J. R. Webber's *Chronicle*, which has been such a help on our journey, offers supportive statistics. W.G.'s 1,478 first-class innings brought him 54,211 runs (including 124 centuries) at an average of 39.45. He also scooped up 2,808 first-class wickets. But that was only half the story. In some 1,066 traced innings in minor cricket he amassed a further 44,556 runs (including 97 more centuries) at an average of 41.40. In minor cricket, too, he took another 4,613 wickets . . . Amplitude, indeed.

* * *

As we stop at the lights at the end of St John's Wood Road, with the Lord's bas-relief on the wall beside us, exhorting everyone to 'Play up! play up! and play the game', many facts and figures jostle for consideration. Like Cardus in 1923, we find images of W.G. coming irresistibly forward. One, in particular, steadily asserts itself: that loyally polished marble grave at Elmers End. As we stop for more traffic lights, we find ourselves back at the fiftieth anniversary in 1965, with a passionate vicar coming slowly into focus, standing by the grave, unbothered by the chill of autumn and his billowing regalia. 'Cricket is a fine game,' cries Neville Sugden in his trenchant, no-nonsense way. 'If it is continued to be played in the same spirit in which W.G. played it – and he really put bat to ball and hit it! – then the future is in good hands, and we may thank God for all those who play the game in England's green and pleasant land.'

The lights have changed. We're on our way again. That image of the 1960s is fading, giving way to another, and we find that, this time – *labuntur anni* – we have made it all the way back to 1915. Thomson's soldier on leave is there at Elmers End, his head full of Tennyson, still meditating in solitude on the death of legendary kings. And on new suns rising, bringing in new years . . .

Selected Bibliography

Allen, David Rayvern (ed.), *Cricket With Grace* (London: Unwin Hyman, 1990)

Ball, Keith, Avery, Bert & Parker, Grahame, *1889: When Play Began at Ashley Down* (Bristol: Gloucestershire C.C.C., 1989)

Bax, Clifford, *W.G. Grace* (London: Phoenix House, 1952)

Bradfield, Donald, *The Lansdown Story* (Bath: Lansdown CC, 1971)

Brownlee, W. Methven, *W.G. Grace* (London: Iliffe, 1887)

Burrell, J. F., *Sides and Squares* (Bristol: Clifton CC, 1983)

Cardus, Neville, *Days in the Sun* (London: Grant Richards, 1924)

Carpenter, Revd Canon Derek, *W.G. Grace* (Dartford: Froude Printing, 1998)

Darwin, Bernard, *W.G. Grace* (London: Duckworth, 1934)

Gordon, Sir Home (with Lord Hawke & Lord Harris) (eds.), *The Memorial Biography of Dr. W.G. Grace* (London: Constable, 1919)

Grace, W.G. (with Brownlee, W. Methven), *Cricket* (Bristol: Arrowsmith, 1891)

Grace, W.G. (with Porritt, Arthur), *'W.G.': Cricketing Reminiscences & Personal Recollections* (London: Bowden, 1899)

Grace, W.G. (with Sewell, E.H.D.), *W.G.'s Little Book* (London: Newnes, 1909)

Green, Stephen (ed.), *The Great Cricketer*, Exhibition catalogue (London, M.C.C. Museum, 1998)

Griffiths, G. J., *King Wakatip* (Dunedin: John McIndoe, 1971)

Jones, Revd Arthur Emlyn, *Our Parish Mangotsfield* (Bristol: Mack, 1899)

Jones, Peris, *Gentlemen & Players* (Bristol: Downend Local History Society, 1989)

Lander, John, *Tent Methodism 1814-1832* (Milton Keynes: Authentic Media, 2003)

Lincoln, Bob, *Reminiscences of Sport in Grimsby* (Grimsby: Grimsby News Co., 1912)

Low, Robert, *W.G. Grace: An Intimate Biography* (London: Richard Cowen, 1997)

Meredith, Anthony, *The Demon & The Lobster* (London: Heinemann, Kingswood, 1987)

Middleton, Judy, *The Royal Brunswick Ground* (Online: Hove, Portslade and Brighton in the Past, 2012)

Midwinter, Eric, *W.G. Grace: His Life & Times* (London: Allen & Unwin, 1981)

Packham, Roger, *Cricket In The Park* (London: Methuen, 2009)

Parker, Grahame, *Gloucestershire Road* (London: Pelham Books, 1983)

Pocock, George, *The Aeropleustic Art* (San Francisco: Edward Sterne, 1969, facsimile of 1827 edition)

Powell, A.G. & Caple, S. Canynge, *The Graces* (London: The Cricket Book Society, 1948)

Powell, Archie & Moore, David, *W.G. Grace Centenary Souvenir Booklet* (Bristol: Gloucestershire C.C.C., 1948)

Rae, Simon, *W.G. Grace* (London: Faber & Faber, 1998)

Rees, Keith (compiler), *The Rees Pocock Connection* (Ballarat, for private circulation, 2011–13)

Rice, Jonathan (ed.), *Wisden on Grace* (London: Bloomsbury, 2015)

Rice, Tim, *Treasures of Lord's* (London: Collins, 1989)

Simons, Grenville, *Lillywhite's Legacy* (Birtsmorton: Wisteria Books, 2004)

Sugden, Revd Neville, *W.G. Grace* (Bromley: privately printed, 1965)

Thomson A.A., *The Great Cricketer* (London: Hutchinson, 1957)

Webber, J.R., *The Chronicle of W.G.* (Nottingham: Association of Cricket Statisticians & Historians, 1998)

Williams, Morley (ed), *Downend Cricket Club 1893-1993* (Bristol: Downend C.C., 1993)

Yates, Edmund (ed.), *Celebrities At Home* first series (London: *The World*, 1877)

About the Author

Anthony Meredith is a widely published author with three previous books on cricket: *The Demon and the Lobster* (Heinemann, 1987), *Summers In Winter* (Methuen 1990) and *Lord's Through Time* (Amberley, 2012). A long-time member of M.C.C., he was for several years a regular contributor to *The Cricketer*. Other interests include music (major biographies on composers Malcolm Arnold, Malcolm Williamson and Richard Rodney Bennett) and dance - he was involved in creating scores for Northern Ballet's *The Three Musketeers* and *The Great Gatsby*. His most recent book for Amberley featured Silverstone's first Grand Prix back in 1948.

Index